TALES *of* ATROCITY *and* RESISTANCE:
First-Person Stories of Teens in the Holocaust

LIFE *in the* NAZI GHETTOS

Hallie Murray and Ann Byers

Enslow Publishing
101 W. 23rd Street
Suite 240
New York, NY 10011
USA
enslow.com

Special thanks to the people of the United States Holocaust Memorial Museum in Washington, DC, for all their help in completing this book.

Published in 2019 by Enslow Publishing, LLC.
101 W. 23rd Street, Suite 240, New York, NY 10011

Cataloging-in-Publication Data

Names: Murray, Hallie. | Byers, Ann.
Title: Life in the Nazi ghettos / Hallie Murray and Ann Byers.
Description: New York : Enslow Publishing, 2019. | Series: Tales of atrocity and resistance: first-person stories of teens in the holocaust | Includes bibliographical references and index. | Audience: Grades 7–12.
Identifiers: ISBN 9780766098343 (pbk.) | ISBN 9780766098336 (library bound)
Subjects: LCSH: Jewish children in the Holocaust—Juvenile literature. | Jewish ghettos—Juvenile literature. | Holocaust, Jewish (1939–1945)—Juvenile literature.
Classification: LCC D804.34 M87 2019 | DDC 940.53/1835083—dc23

Printed in the United States of America

Portions of this book originally appeared in *Trapped—Youth in the Nazi Ghettos* by Ann Byers.

Photo Credits: Cover, pp. 3, 35, 37 Imagno/Hulton Archive/Getty Images; pp. 4, 7, 50, 82–83 Keystone/Hulton Archive/Getty Images; p. 10 David E. Scherman/The LIFE Picture Collection/Getty Images; p. 13 Taussig/Hulton Archive/Getty Images; p. 15 Corbis Historical/Getty Images; pp. 16–17, 89 Bettmann/Getty Images; pp. 20, 45, 108–109 Galerie Bilderwelt/Hulton Archive/Getty Images; p. 22 Private Collection/© Look and Learn/Bridgeman Images; pp. 24–25, 30–31, 42 Universal Images Group/Getty Images; pp. 29, 66, 98–99 © AP Images; p. 32 Paul Fearn/Alamy Stock Photo; pp. 40–41 Fox Photos/Hulton Archive/Getty Images; pp. 48–49 Hugo Jaeger/The LIFE Picture Collection/Getty Images; p. 53 United States Holocaust Memorial Museum, courtesy of Rafal Imbro; pp. 56–57 United States Holocaust Memorial Museum, courtesy of Jan Kostanski; p. 61 United States Holocaust Memorial Museum, courtesy of Miep Koenig-de-Zwarte; p. 63 United States Holocaust Memorial Museum, courtesy of Eliezer Zilberis; p. 65 ullstein bild/Getty Images; pp. 68–69 Sueddeutsche Zeitung Photo/Alamy Stock Photo; pp. 76–77 The LIFE Picture Collection/Getty Images; p. 79 United States Holocaust Memorial Museum, courtesy of George Kadish/Zvi Kadushin; p. 85 © SZ Photo/Bridgeman Images; p. 94 Hulton Archive/Archive Photos/Getty Images; pp. 100–101 Sueddeutsche Zeitung Photo/Alamy Stock Photo; pp. 104–105 United States Holocaust Memorial Museum, courtesy of Leah Hammerstein Silverstein; p. 106 Sovfoto/Universal Images Group/Getty Images; cover and interior pages graphic elements kikujungboy/Shutterstock.com (barbed wire), ghenadie/Shutterstock.com (Star of David).

Contents

Introduction

World War I, which lasted from 1914 to 1918, devastated much of Europe, but Germany was, in many ways, hit the hardest. Germany, as the German Empire, had fought alongside the Ottoman Empire and the Austro-Hungarian Empire against the Allied Powers, including France, Britain, Russia, and the United States, and badly lost. The terms of the peace treaty, the Versailles Treaty, forced Germany to admit full responsibility for the war and to bear the costs the victors incurred in the fighting. Germany had also lost almost 2.5 million people, large chunks of its territory and most of its military might. The German economy had also been severely damaged by the vast financial stress of maintaining the military, reparations paid after the war's end, and the Great Depression of the 1930s, which affected countries across the world. The German people were afraid and angry, and they wanted things to change as quickly as possible.

Many Germans believed Adolf Hitler and his political allies were the answer to Germany's problems. A fiery orator, Hitler promised German citizens a restored, glorious Germany in the near future and offered them a scapegoat for their present problems: the Jewish people of Germany. In much of Europe, especially Eastern Europe, anti-Semitism was deeply rooted. Throughout the nineteenth century, Jews were frequently the targets of prejudice, misunderstanding, and a number of bloody riots, called pogroms. Furthermore, conspiracy theories abounded after the Second World War, and many people were easily convinced that Germany had lost because they had been sabotaged from the inside by Jews and other ethnic minorities within the country.

Hitler convinced many Germans that the Jews were the source of their country's problems. After joining the fledgling Nazi Party in 1919, he molded it into a political force driven by violence and anti-Semitism—hatred of the Jews. His ultimate goal was to rule a German empire that stretched across all of Europe, an empire that would be inhabited by Aryans—what Hitler called the Germanic peoples. But nine million Jews lived among the "Aryans" and other people in the land he wanted. What would he do with them?

As Hitler rose to power, the Nazis wrestled with this question for some time. Their eventual answer was to simply get rid of them. They began by stripping Jews of their rights, systematically taking away their political power, then their financial power as Jews were removed from their jobs, and finally their basic human rights. The Nazis eventual plan, which began in 1941, was to murder all of Europe's Jews in what the Nazi leaders called the "final solution." Such a monstrous goal would have to be achieved in stages. First, they would separate the Jews from everyone else: the ghettos were created to hold Jews in one place until Nazi soldiers could move them to death

Adolf Hitler was the leader of Germany from 1933 until his suicide at the end of World War II in 1945. He had a unique style of oration, and his speeches compelled many Germans to commit anti-Semitic violence during his time as chancellor.

camps, where they would be killed en masse. Some people escaped; many others died in the ghettos or even before ghettos were created. But for the most part, ghettos helped Nazi soldiers keep Jews all together until they could begin their program of mass murder.

Chapter 1

Creating the Ghettos

In post-World War I Europe, anti-Semitism ran rampant, and the Nazi initiative to blame Jews for Germany's problems in the years following the war was incredibly successful. As Hitler rose to power, Jews were increasingly persecuted by both the German government and by German citizens. (At this point, Jews were no longer even considered German citizens). As Germany expanded its reach, Jews and other "undesirable" minorities like the Romani were forcibly isolated from Aryans in order to achieve the Nazi dream of an Aryan empire.

On September 1, 1939, Germany invaded Poland, beginning the conflict that would eventually become World War II. Even in the early stages of the war, German soldiers hunted down Jewish civilians. In the early days of the war, Jewish men in particular were targets of terrorism and violence, although all Jews were treated poorly by Nazi soldiers. Harold Zissman lived in a Polish town near the German border. He described what happened in the first days of German occupation:

> At four in the afternoon . . . German soldiers—weapons aimed, fingers on triggers, hollering orders—drove all the Jewish men out of their homes. Downstairs we were lined up six abreast and marched to the public high school. The brutes with their rifles and truncheons beat anyone who fell behind. They made us empty our pockets of all personal items. Machine-gun outposts guarded the school building and yard; German soldiers with mounted bayonets were stationed around the complex. The ferocity with which these barbarians treated us—innocent, helpless men—was deeply dispiriting. Suddenly all attention was directed to the balcony, where a tall German officer in a crisp uniform with gleaming buttons shouted at us—first in German, then in Polish—that everyone must observe the curfew from 6 P.M. to 7 A.M. Those who didn't would be shot. After six in the evening, we were finally released, and we ran home under a hail of machine-gun bullets.[1]

Methods of Identification

After the Nazi soldiers took over Poland, Germany sent in the Gestapo—the secret police of the Nazi state—in order to begin the process of isolating Jews.

First, however, they had to identify them. During the annual meeting of the Nazi Party at Nuremberg in 1935, the all-Nazi German parliament had passed laws that defined a "Jew" as someone who was more than half Jewish. These laws also stripped Jews of many rights, including the right to vote, the right to marry someone non-Jewish, and the right to be a citizen of Germany at all. Yet as Nazi Germany expanded, they needed a new way to easily tell Jews apart from non-Jews. Zissman explained how the Nazis distinguished between the two in Poland:

The Gestapo offices are marked by the word "Gestapo," an abbreviation of Geheime Staatspolizei, meaning "secret state police." The swastika further indicates their association with the Nazi Party.

> The German[s] . . . would post posters on lighting poles or whatsoever, wherever posters could be posted, telling the new ordinance . . . that the Jews must be identified and must carry identification and in the early part, at least in our city, we were supposed to wear a band with the . . . Star of David on it. And it was told immediately if one is caught, they will be shot. That was for anything that one violates . . . [such as the] curfew. . . . It was immediately declared that Jews cannot walk on sidewalks. So, the identity was the arm band and you must not walk on the sidewalk; you must walk just on the streets.[2]

The Star of David badge or armband was first required in Poland. The Nazis forced Jews to wear the symbol as an identifying marker. When the German army moved from Poland to cities of Western Europe, Jews there also had to wear the identifying badge. In May 1942, Jews in Holland were commanded to wear the emblem. It separated sixteen-year-old Edward Lessing from his half-Jewish cousin as they walked the streets of Delft:

> All Jews had to wear a star if they went out of the house. So my mother sewed on stars on my clothes. And I remember an incident. I have a cousin. . . . He's about my age, and at the time we looked a little bit similar. And we had both gotten the same overcoats from my father's former clothing store, so we looked like twins. And Hans always said, "Let's go out and walk like twins." So we put on the same socks, shirt, much as possible . . . same outfit and we walked as twins. . . .
>
> That was wonderful. Except I had a star. He didn't. Well, that was the only thing different. . . . His mother . . . my Aunt Clara, had married a non-Jew. So Hans was only half-Jewish. . . .

> We were stopped by this German in our same overcoats. And the German said to my cousin, Hans, "What're you do[ing] walking with a Jew?"
>
> And I said, "He's my cousin."
>
> And the German slapped me full in the face and I fell on the ground. Pow. . . . He said something like "You lousy Jew." And he said to my cousin, "Don't let me ever see you walking with him . . . with a Jew."[3]

The Jewish badge became mandatory in France in June 1942.

The Nazis punished children harshly if they were caught without the identifying mark. Fifteen-year-old Helene Baraf later wrote about the punishment:

> My brother had a birthday in July...and for his birthday my mother bought him a trench coat. And this trench coat, unfortunately, cost him his life. . . . One day when he was playing [chess in a café] . . . the Gestapo came and asked, "To whom does belong that trench coat?"
>
> And my . . . brother stupidly answered, "It's mine." And there was no Jewish cross, Star of David, on it, so they took him to jail.
>
> My mother immediately went to the Gestapo. She . . . begged him to release him . . . telling him it was . . . a mistake. He had it on his suit, the Star of David, but not on the coat. . . . But nothing doing. They wouldn't release him. He stayed in jail in Loos. . . . From there they sent him . . . to [the death camp] Auschwitz.[4]

Separation and Isolation

After identifying the Jews, the Nazis set about trying to separate them from non-Jews. Eventually, Nazis planned to send Jews and others, like political prisoners, to the killing

A Jewish couple walking on the street in Prague, Czechoslovakia. Whenever they were in public, Jews were forced to wear yellow patches in the shape of the Star of David, like the one on this man's coat.

centers that were to be built in Poland. Until those centers were operational, the Jews were confined to specific areas so they could be moved easily when the time was right. In the conquered cities of Western Europe, they were held in transit camps. In the east, they were herded into small areas in certain cities. Emanuel Tanay was only fourteen when the Jewish ghetto was formed in his city just south of Krakow, Poland:

> One day there came an announcement that there will be a Jewish quarters, which has come to be known as the ghetto. But they, the Germans, called it the Jewish quarters. . . . It gave you a perimeter where Jews could live, which was a tiny portion of the town. And I'm

The Gestapo and the SS

Over the course of the 1920s, more and more Nazis were elected to German Parliament until the only represented party was that of the Nazis. At that point, with the nomination of Hitler as the German Chancellor in 1933, Germany became a fascist state, and it was decreed that the only political party would be the Nazi Party. In order to stay in power and achieve their goals, Nazis also created a few different militarized groups. One of these was the Gestapo, the secret state police of Germany. Another was the Schutzstaffel, or SS, which began as a secret guard for Hitler and high-ranking Nazis, and eventually became a major force under Hitler's control. Both the Gestapo and the SS helped control, hurt, and murder Jews and other groups considered disposable by the Nazi regime.

Heinrich Himmler was the leader of the Schutzstaffel (SS) and a key member of the Nazi Party leadership.

> speaking of the town where I lived [Miechow], but it was similarly true in other towns. And the Poles who lived in that area had to evacuate. But there was no problem because . . . the area that the Jews left was a much wider one. So whatever Pole was displaced from the Jewish-designated area . . . they got much better quarters anyway, but not the other way around.[5]

In several cities, the local authorities helped the Gestapo imprison the Jews. Some were paid for their assistance and some, like the Nazis, were anti-Semitic.

When Germany invaded Hungary in 1944, fourteen-year-old Madeline Deutsch watched as the Hungarians of her own town helped establish the ghetto there:

> The German SS . . . with total cooperation of the Hungarian police and the Hungarian gendarmes, came to our homes very early in the morning, at dawn. And knocking real hard, and "Jews, get out of your house. Get out and line up in front of the house." We couldn't imagine what was happening. I mean, it was just a horrible, horrible thing. The children were screaming,

Police in Berlin complete an investigation of a Jewish home in 1933. German police would search Jewish homes looking for incriminating documents and weapons and arrest anyone suspected of plotting against the government.

> and all of us were . . . afraid. We didn't know what was happening and what was to come.[6]

As the Jews were pushed into the ghettos, Deutsch recalled, they could take very little with them:

> We were told that we'll be allowed back to the house for just a few minutes to get a little suitcase or a little handbag in which we could put a . . . change of clothing and maybe some food, just dry food like a piece of bread or something that we had. And then we were to come out again and line up in front of . . . our homes. So we each got a little bag and put just the bare minimum in there. And then we were being marched down the streets where there was the small ghetto.[7]

Often, even what they tried to take along was cruelly wrenched from them. When Regina Hamburger Bomba was moved to the ghetto of Radomsko, Poland, in 1940, the twenty-year-old stood in horror: "The Nazis came in to take us. . . . It was . . . one o'clock at night. . . . They took away our money, our possessions. They took off a ring from my mother . . . with the flesh."[8]

Limited Space

The ghettos were horribly overcrowded. Still, the Gestapo tried to squeeze additional people into them. When no more could be crowded in, the Nazis had no trouble disposing of those who could not fit. When German soldiers entered Siauliai, Lithuania, they took about one thousand Jewish men to the Kuziai forest and shot them. Within the next two months, the rest of the Jews were marched to two newly formed ghettos. Thirteen-year-old Nesse Galperin Godin was one of the "lucky" ones who made it in:

> To go into the ghetto you just had to show the certificate. If you had the certificate, they let you in through the gate. So about five thousand people got into the ghetto. We had ten thousand Jewish people into the two ghettos. The people that did not get the . . . certificate—I believe it's about 3,500 of them—the orphanage, the old-age home, the elderly, the sick, the children from many families, and many, many people . . . they were put into the city synagogues. . . . They were begging for food, they were begging . . . to be saved. People were trying—our Jewish community council, who were wonderful people, they tried so hard to save [them]. . . . These people were killed just like the thousand men, in another forest—3,500 of them. So by the time the ghetto was formed . . . half of our population was killed.[9]

Large-scale murder was often the prelude to the ghetto. In Vilna, Lithuania, the section that the Nazis selected for the ghetto was too small for the forty thousand people of the city and surrounding areas. To fit as many as possible, the Nazis needed to eliminate five to ten thousand Jews. Rochelle Blackman Slivka, nineteen when the Vilna ghetto was formed in 1941, knew how the Germans made room:

> There was a poor section where a lot of . . . poor Jews lived. . . . And one night, the SS, with the help of the Ukrainian police with the Lithuanians, they came in and took out all the Jews from there and they drove them to a place, Ponary, outskirts of Vilna there, and they shot them all there. We heard screaming and yelling and crying during the night, but we weren't allowed to look out of the window, because those who looked out were shot. We didn't know what was going on anyway until the next day our neighbors told us what was going on. . . . And a couple of weeks later they rounded up all

In this 1942 image from the Lodz ghetto, the man in the foreground is easily identified as Jewish from the yellow Star of David on his jacket. The Lodz ghetto was the second-largest ghetto in Poland after Warsaw.

> the Jews from the city and the suburbs and they put us all in this ghetto.[10]

The very first ghetto established during the Holocaust was constructed not far from Lodz, Poland, only a month after the beginning of the war. In the next five years, more than 1.5 million Jews were imprisoned in more than one thousand ghettos in Eastern Europe. Most of the ghettos were in cities where Jews already lived and where Jews from nearby villages could be brought. Many were created near railroad lines, by which the residents could be easily transported to labor or death camps. Most Jews of the ghettos died either there or in the camps.

Chapter 2

Relocation, Isolation, and Imprisonment

Though ghettos ranged in size and duration, most ghettos were established according to the same pattern. The origins of the word "ghetto" aren't clear, but it was initially used in sixteenth century Italy to describe the place in Venice where Jews were forced to lived.

In order to create ghettos in the Second World War, Nazis would first evacuate people from the oldest, poorest, most rundown part of a city. Then all the Jews were ordered to move into the newly cleared section. In some places, they were given barely enough time to get their things together before they were forced to move from their homes into the buildings in the ghetto. Jews in Krakow, Poland, for example, were given seventeen days to relocate. Amalie Petranker Salsitz's parents had lived in a nice home, and the nineteen-year-old could not believe she would have to leave:

> We were told that we will have to leave our apartment and move to a section which was designated as ghetto. This was the poorest section of the Jews. . . . My parents

The word "ghetto" comes from the the area of Venice where Jews were made to live in the sixteenth century. This nineteenth-century engraving shows an English interpretation of what a Venetian ghetto may have looked like.

> secured immediately an apartment in the future ghetto, and the always optimist Jew . . . we hoped the war will end before we'll have to move. We transferred our furniture there. We still kept only a mattress . . . with hope that we'll maybe not have to move.[1]

But when the deadline came, their hopes were dashed: "We were in our apartment which almost was bare. . . . Only the mattresses and some utensils. We heard terrible commotion and noise. I went out on the balcony and I saw a lot of Gestapo and Ukrainian police. We knew something is brewing, something bad is going [to happen]."[2]

The Relocation

The move into the ghetto was a universally bad experience. German soldiers could be incredibly cruel and violent as they forced Jews to move from their homes into the poor sections of the city. They often broke valuables, used slurs and taunts, and destroyed homes. Twelve-year-old Nina Kaleska never forgot the horror of moving to the ghetto of Grodno, Poland:

> The entire Jewish population of Grodno was being uprooted from their home and that I remember very distinctly and with great pain. We had some beautiful china. We had a very lovely home. Wasn't rich, but it was beautiful. The Germans would come in and simply at the whim of a wisp, just like that [fingers snap], remove the most beautiful china and just throw it against a wall to break it, for fun, and started to taunt and tease. And you didn't really have to be old or young to recognize that this was the devil in the flesh.[3]

If people were not moving to their new quarters quickly enough, the Nazis used ruthless prods. Fifteen-year-old

A Jewish policeman and a Nazi soldier direct people across the street in the Lodz ghetto. The Nazi soldier is to the left, identifiable by the swastika on the arm of his uniform. The sign above the street reads "Residential Area of the Jews. Do Not Enter."

DER

Michael Etkind described his move to the ghetto in Lodz, Poland:

> Three days before the final date for leaving for the ghetto, there were raids and many Jews . . . were shot inside their dwellings. This was designed to stampede the Jewish population into leaving for the "safety" of the ghetto. Needless to say, it succeeded. During the next three days, thousands upon thousands of makeshift sleighs could be seen converging on the ghetto area, loaded with bundles of bedding. The ground was frozen and there was a blizzard blowing as I was pulling my sledge filled with our belongings. My mother, . . . my younger sister and my little brother . . . were pushing from behind. We made a number of journeys. . . . There were three adults and five children in a room of about 250 square feet.[4]

Fifteen-year-old Irena Aronowicz remembered the event in Lodz as very chaotic: "Everyone was going in the same direction, rushing toward the same goal, the dirtiest, ugliest quarter of the city, a place with no sewers and paved with cobblestones."[5]

Anti-Semitism was not limited to Nazi soldiers, and many of the non-Jewish Poles could be equally cruel. Seventeen-year-old Lily Margules saw such harshness in Vilna:

> When we came to the ghetto, it was a very terrible experience because we were carrying with us our meager possessions and the Poles lined up on the street and when they saw somebody of us wearing two coats, they used to say, "Aw, look at this Jew. She is . . . wearing two coats. Let's take one of them off." And they would just grab and take it away, and . . . nobody even interfered.[6]

Ghettos Throughout Europe

There were hundreds of ghettos across Eastern Europe, but they varied greatly in size and duration. Some were large and some were small, depending on the number of Jews living in the surrounding area. The largest was in Warsaw, Poland and held about four hundred thousand people. Some ghettos lasted only a few weeks, just long enough to transport Jews to the camps. Many of the larger ones stood for years. It took time for the death camps to handle so many, and the Germans utilized the ghettos as a source of Jewish labor for the war effort. Since most Jews had been forcibly relocated, the Nazis patrolling the ghettos controlled their lives and livelihoods, and for many the only work available went toward helping the German military.

A Safe Space?

As harsh as the move to the ghettos was, some of the Jews in Poland were actually relieved when it was announced. In earlier times, Jews had lived in their own communities, in ghettos, and they had felt safe there. Some thought these ghettos would be a shelter from the abuse of their conquerors. Before the ghettos were established, Nazi officials and local authorities could order Jews to do demeaning and backbreaking work whenever they wished. And they could beat or even shoot Jews at will. Amalie Petranker Salsitz saw the brutality in Krakow:

> We saw shooting on the street, random shooting. They took the Jews . . . to work on the street. They used to

> catch them, you know, and then to dig ditches or to work at bridges and then sometimes they used to throw them into the river and Russians erected many monuments, so [the Germans] took the Jews to destroy the monuments, and many of them were shot.[7]

Teenagers were especially vulnerable. Ben Helfgott, barely ten when he was shut up in the ghetto of Piotrkow, Poland, witnessed and experienced the violence:

> Young people suffered. From fifteen onwards, they could not walk in the streets for fear of being taken for forced labour. In mid-1940, 200–250 were rounded up and taken to build fortifications on the River Bug. . . . Our nights weren't safe either. The police would knock on the doors at night to round up young people to be taken away for forced labour.[8]

The ghetto was not any safer than the streets of the occupied cities. When asked if there were beatings in her ghetto, Sonia Heidocovsky Zissman replied, "They don't have to beat you. They kill you right there and then."[9]

The killings served to frighten the people into submission. In the early days, fear kept Jews in the ghettos. Ben Helfgott observed that in the Piotrkow ghetto, "there was no real rule that anyone that went out of the ghetto would be shot. Some would be shot, some would be beaten."[10] But the risk of being shot made leaving the ghetto a risk no one was really prepared to take.

Open and Closed

Some of the ghettos, such as Piotrkow, began as "open ghettos." This meant that they had no walls or fences, but the Nazis controlled who could enter and who could

This image of the Szydlow ghetto in Poland was taken in 1940. The man in the background wears a white armband, which all Jews over the age of ten were required to wear.

leave. Few of the ghettos remained open like this for long. Fourteen-year-old Emanuel Tanay saw the sudden closure of the Miechow ghetto outside Krakow: "Once you were there, suddenly one day they put up walls separating the ghetto from the rest. . . . Brick walls. They built a . . . large brick wall with a small gate that opened up and the ghetto was completely cut off from the rest of town."[11]

Some of the ghetto walls were brick; others were made of barbed wire. Some ghettos had wooden fences and some

Ghetto residents were often forced to perform hard labor. Here, Jewish inmates build a brick wall to create the boundary of the ghetto in Krakow, Poland.

had stone barricades. Some walls were topped with broken glass. The wall of the Krakow ghetto was made partly of gravestones torn out of Jewish cemeteries. Always, the residents in the ghetto had to erect their own walls. Fourteen-year-old Abraham Malnik helped build the wall at Kovno, Lithuania: "They grabbed people to make the fences. I was also one to make a fence. And we had to encircle ourselves in our own fence."[12]

While the walls were going up, the Nazis did not want the people to panic—not just yet. Emanuel Tanay felt relatively free in Miechow at first: "They didn't say you couldn't leave [the ghetto]. You could leave; you couldn't leave it after 6:00. There was a curfew, but up to a certain point, you could just walk into town and walk and so on." But once the ghetto walls were up, Tanay said, "Jews could not leave the ghetto at all except by special permit."[13]

Thus, very soon after they were formed, most of the ghettos were closed. The Jews inside them were sealed off from the outside world. Tanay described the sealing of Miechow as a gradual but rapid process:

> The Jews moved in, few families into one room; two families, maybe one family in one room in the beginning. Because the ghetto . . . the Jewish . . . part of town would become smaller and smaller and smaller. But at first it was open, so you could get in and out in certain hours. For example . . . a Jew could not be in the street after seven o'clock. But all the other times you could get out and mingle, be outside. One day there was an announcement: the ghetto is closed. And there were gates. There were walls built, and you couldn't get out. So, you see, there was this ever-increasing . . . level of persecution.[14]

Inside the Walls

Although the imprisonment occurred in stages in many towns, the final blow—the sealing of the ghettos—fell quite

Yitskhok Rudashevski appears here above his grandmother and two cousins. He wrote of his experiences in the Vilna ghetto as a teenager during the Holocaust.

suddenly. Tosha Bialer described the closing of the ghetto of Warsaw, Poland:

> There was no way out any more. . . . Suddenly, the realization struck us. What had been, up till now, seemingly unrelated parts—a piece of wall here, a blocked-up house there, another piece of wall somewhere else—had overnight been joined to form an enclosure from which there was no escape. . . . Like cattle we had been herded into the corral, and the gate had been barred behind us.[15]

Once the ghettos were sealed, there was almost no escape. Sixteen-year-old David Lieberman could not leave

Czestochowa, Poland, after August 23, 1941: "They locked the ghetto in. You couldn't get in, get out. All the streets were locked with the Gestapo."[16]

How did children react to the chaos, the restriction, and the terror? Thirteen-year-old Yitskhok Rudashevski wrote in his diary about the establishment and sealing of the Vilna ghetto:

> The streets are closed off. . . . The streets are turbulent. . . . A ghetto is being created for Vilna Jews. People are packing. . . . The women go back and forth. They wring their hands. . . . I go around with bleary eyes among the bundles, see how we are being uprooted overnight from our home. Soon we have our first view of the move to the ghetto . . . a gray black mass of people goes harnessed to large bundles. . . .
>
> People fall, bundles scatter. . . . [They] drive us on, do not let us rest. I think of nothing: not what I am losing, not what I have just lost, not what is in store for me. I do not see the streets before me, the people passing by. I only feel that I am terribly weary, I feel that . . . a hurt is burning inside me. . . . I feel that . . . my freedom is being robbed from me, my home, and the familiar Vilna streets I love so much. I have been cut off from all that is dear and precious to me. . . .
>
> The little streets are still full of a restless mass of people. It is hard to push your way through. I feel as if I were in a box. There is no air to breathe. Wherever you go you encounter a gate that hems you in.[17]

The bleary eyes, the weariness, and the hurt burning inside—these were only the beginning. Worse troubles were yet to come.

Chapter 3

"Life Goes On"

Though moving to the ghetto was certainly a traumatic experience, some people viewed it as simply the next injustice in a long line of anti-Semitic acts committed by a European government. Anti-Semitism had been alive and well in Europe even before the Nazis gained power, and although the scale and intensity of persecution increased dramatically when they invaded, it was not an entirely new experience.

Those who were sent to the ghettos and unable to escape worked hard to make the best of their situation, especially for the children. They didn't necessarily know what was coming, that the Nazis were prepared to kill everyone when they were able. Many people found the only possible way to cope was to try to carve out a life in the ghetto as best they could. Life had to continue somehow.

Fourteen-year-old Emanuel Tanay experienced this attitude soon after moving to the ghetto of Miechow, Poland:

> You know the amazing thing is that life goes on, particularly for . . . children, even under those dreadful

Jews of all ages made their home in the ghettos. Although life in the ghettos was very difficult, people still managed to find joy in things. This little boy lived in the Warsaw ghetto around 1943, and here he holds a piece of cake.

> circumstances. You know, I do recall that my friends and I would play in the ghetto and . . . there were certain activities that were exciting. Adventuresome even. . . . Life went on even though it seems all so dreadful. But people played, people even got married, at first, and had children and so on. Life went on.[1]

Thomas Buergenthal, almost six years old at the time, recalled that coping in the ghetto of Kielce, Poland, became more difficult with each passing day:

> Initially [after the German invasion of Poland] . . . things were not all that bad.
>
> It was when the ghetto was established, all the Jews were herded into one part of the city. Food became very scarce. Housing became very scarce. We lived in one room that my father and mother and I shared. And food was very difficult to come by.
>
> A lot of hunger, but still not as serious. There were still a lot of people who lived quite well, who had ways of getting food into the ghetto, especially in the beginning. Things gradually became harder and harder.[2]

When the ghettos were sealed, life in general became much more difficult. People could not go in and out of the ghetto, they could not work at their old jobs, and they could not get food the way they had in the past. Twenty-one-year-old Eva Rozencwajig found the ghetto of Kozienice, Poland, miserable: "We were already very scared. . . . [At] one time we were a middle-class family . . . and [when we went into the ghetto] we stopped living. We had to fight for the every day . . . to get the food on the table. . . . [We were] afraid to go out. They're shooting people."[3]

Disease Spreads

The crowded conditions made life particularly difficult. A huge number of people were crammed into a small area, a situation that has historically led to sickness, starvation, and sometimes disagreements and violence. Nine-year-old Hanka Ziegler did not like sharing a room in the ghetto of Piotrkow with her family and with strangers: "We all [parents and siblings] stayed in one little room, the seven of us. Another 14 people came to the room at different times. . . . I remember sleeping on a chair with one of my brothers. It was awful."[4]

In the cramped quarters, sicknesses spread quickly. Diseases raged through the ghettos.

Poor living conditions and close quarters meant that disease spread easily in the ghettos. This Jewish doctor, identifiable by the black Star of David on his coat, gives children medical examinations in the Warsaw ghetto around 1940.

The most deadly disease was typhus, a highly contagious, often lethal condition that was frequently spread by lice. Stefan Ernest, who probably perished in the Warsaw ghetto, left a chilling account of the effect of the disease:

> [In the Warsaw ghetto] in the summer of 1941, an epidemic of typhus broke out in full fury. . . . The epidemic was to last unchecked for almost a year. . . . At the beginning there were several dozen deaths daily, and in the months when it was at its worst . . . it yielded 200 corpses daily.[5]

The doctors in the ghettos tried to help the sick, but they were unable to get medicines. So the very mention of the disease struck fear in the hearts of all the ghetto residents. Claudia Royter Liberchuk was a very small child when she first heard the deadly word: "I remember how they [let us in the cellar] and somebody was on the bed, and somebody pronounced *typhuses*, you know, the sickness. . . . They left immediately. . . . This I remember there was a magic word. *Typhus* was a magic word."[6]

The word *typhus* was feared for good reason. The disease was painful and, in the ghettos, often fatal. Florence Gittelman Eisen was fourteen when she came down with it in the Lachwa ghetto in southern Russia:

> I got temperature. . . . And I start to vomit blood. . . . And they put me [with] . . . dead people. . . . Some alive, some dead, some dying from the typhus. And I was so sick that they put me there already. . . . There was laying dead people from—dying on typhus. . . . I crawled off that . . . bed. It was a bed for 25 people probably. I crawled out of the house. . . . I crawled out, I went behind the barn and I lay down there to die. All by myself.[7]

Fortunately for Florence, her father rescued her and nursed her back to health. Countless others were not so lucky.

The Threat of Starvation

As feared as disease was, it was not the major concern of the Jews of the ghettos. The issue that consumed all of them, young and old, was finding food. Emanuel Tanay had a very hard time getting food in the Miechow ghetto:

> Food was a tremendous problem because, you see, even the Polish population [outside the ghetto] had starvation type of rationing and the Jews were given virtually no food. So you had to, through black market activities, bring the food from the Polish side into the ghetto. And that was again, very, very difficult and once again, punishable by death. For example, bread that wasn't that black type . . . sort of a watery black ration bread—if you had any other bread, and it was found in your home, you would be shot for that. Meat, you would get shot for that.[8]

Nelly Zygler Cesana felt the pangs of hunger in the Warsaw ghetto at age six: "The hunger—I would sit in our apartment and look out the window, and I would see the Polish children across the street bringing milk back home. It was like watching people in a storybook—we had no food, no milk."[9]

The prospect of starvation was so real that teenagers in the Lodz ghetto wrote of the constant hunger in their diaries. When children were still allowed to attend school, thirteen-year-old Chaim Benzion Cale admitted, "I wanted to go to school not so much to learn, but to eat the soup and not be frozen."[10]

Jewish children stand in line for food rations in the Warsaw ghetto in Poland in 1941. Food was very scarce in the ghettos, and starvation was an ever-present danger.

The meager portions of food that children could get at school were not always enough. In the Lodz ghetto, sixteen-year-old Dawid Sierakowiak wrote: "A student from the same grade as ours died from hunger and exhaustion yesterday. As a result of his terrible appearance, he was allowed to eat as much soup in school as he wanted, but it didn't help him much. He is the third victim in the class."[11]

Food was so precious in the ghetto that children ordered their days according to when—and if—they ate. Fourteen-

year-old Sara Rachela Plagier wrote: "In the [Lodz] ghetto we had no need for a calendar. Our lives were divided into periods based on the distribution of food: bread every eighth day, the ration once a month. Each day fell into two parts: before and after we received our soup. In this way the time passed."[12]

The tiny rations were never adequate. An unnamed girl in Lodz confided the pain of hunger to her diary:

> When it's so cold, even my heart is heavy. There is nothing to cook today; we should be receiving three loaves of bread but we will be getting only one bread today. I don't know what to do. I bought rotten and stinking beets from a woman, for 10 marks. We will cook half today and half tomorrow. Does this deserve to be called life?[13]

Senseless Shootings

Hunger was the gnawing nightmare of the ghettos, but one terror was even greater. When asked what she was most afraid of, Sonia Heidocovsky Zissman answered, "Any day they can kill you. What else?!"[14]

Killings occurred not just any day, but nearly every day. Thomas Buergenthal remembered, "In the [Kielce] ghetto itself there were—if not daily, certainly sporadic—killings

Arthur Greiser, a politician of the Nazi Party and leader in the SS, salutes Nazi troops after the Battle of Lodz. Greiser is at the far right, while his soldiers march through the street on horses.

going on by Germans of people, German guards of Jews on the street."[15]

Thirteen-year-old Israel Unikowski saw these killings in the Lodz ghetto: "From this day every German may shoot as many Jews as he wants. If anybody came near the wire fence, as far as his rifle could reach, he could shoot him. Hundreds and hundreds of people perished in the ghetto this way."[16]

Children as well as adults could be killed for the smallest so-called crime. Fourteen-year-old Emanuel Tanay made a game of counting his crimes in the Miechow ghetto:

> Almost everything you did was punishable by death, o.k.? So, you know it's interesting how children, youngsters react. I remember that I and my friends would count how many death penalties we would incur for what we were doing. For example, we would go outside of the ghetto without an arm band; after you were 13 you had to have an arm band. So, it was death penalty for walking without an arm band, death penalty for leaving the ghetto, death penalty for being [outside] after 6:00.[17]

Often the Nazis would go looking for Jews to kill. Tanay recalled the fear the very presence of a German in the ghetto aroused:

> There was one well-known . . . Gestapo character who would come into the ghetto and at random walk into a house, and if he found certain things, he would shoot the person who was the head of the house. . . . There was a tremendous terror when one of those characters would walk into the ghetto, which [used to be], you know, teeming with humanity in the streets. There was no traffic of any kind. . . . The street would be deserted. There would be nobody . . . no sign of life.[18]

Children lived in constant fear. At thirteen, Chaim Benzion Cale could not escape the fear:

> We were scared of all of it. We were scared of Jewish policemen. We were scared of Biebow [the chief German in Lodz]. We were scared of Rumkowski [the chief Jew in the Lodz ghetto]. We were scared of Sonderkommando [Jewish groups assigned to special operations]. We were scared—always we were scared.[19]

And yet, in the midst of the fear and the death, life went on . . . at least for a while.

Chapter 4

Finding a Way to Survive

The situation in the ghettos quickly became desperate, and people sought out any way possible to stay alive. Many found work in the ghettos laboring on behalf of the Nazi military effort. While the death camps were being built, Nazis found that ghetto residents could be a valuable source of slave labor. Among other things, Jews could manufacture products for the German cause, so the Nazis set up workshops in the ghettos. Others worked as servants, either for Nazis or in the ghetto itself, and others still performed manual labor, including digging graves for Russian soldiers and sometimes their fellow Jews. Because working Jews were valuable to the Nazis in many ways, those who could labor were usually the last to be killed. According to the Nazis, however, all were intended to die in the end.

Liquidating the Ghettos

The ghettos were organized around work and death. The large ghettos were divided into two parts: numbers 1 and 2, ghettos A and B, upper and lower, or big and small. One

Children from the Lodz ghetto are directed toward a train that will take them to the Chelmno death camp in September 1942. At that point, ghetto residents were unaware these trains were headed toward extermination camps.

of the two housed the people who were able to work. The other held those who could not work—people of no use to Germany. These would be the first to be killed when the time came.

That time arrived at the beginning of 1942. By then, the first death camp—in Chelmno, Poland—had begun operation. The first mass killing took place on December 8, 1941. Three other camps would open that same year, and two concentration camps would install gas chambers and become death camps. The smoke of war was thick enough to hide the mass murder from people in Western countries who might object. So the Nazi final solution was in full operation in 1942.

The Nazi leaders planned to liquidate the ghettos—to remove all the Jews from the ghettos and dispose of them at the death camps. Yet killing nine million people could not be done all at once. Therefore, the ghettos were emptied in stages. A few hundred or a few thousand people at a time would be selected to go. At first, the residents did not understand where or why they were going, as Nazis intentionally deceived them in order to minimize panic and escape attempts. Dawid Sierakowiak wrote in his diary, "No one knows what happened to the Jews deported from Lodz. No one can be certain of anything now. They are after Jews all over the Reich [Germany and German-occupied territory]."[1]

Some even thought the selected Jews were going somewhere different, maybe even better. Eve Wagszul Rich wrote: "When the first order was to get the Jews out of town, they didn't tell us they were going to kill them. They told us they were going to take the men to labor camps and the women were going to go to a different town."[2]

Even when people were murdered right in front of them, many Jews believed the Nazi lies. Fourteen-year-old Abraham Malnik realized later that the lies were excuses:

> [Kovno consisted of] two ghettos in fact, a small ghetto where they had a little hospital and they put the old people in the hospital, and then there was a large ghetto. . . . They decided to liquidate the hospital and liquidate the doctors and just burn the whole thing up

> . . . and didn't let anybody to go and help them. We were standing outside watching how the sick people and the people are burning up . . . the whole [small] ghetto. And we asked them questions: "How come you do that?" . . .
>
> They give us all kinds of excuses that from now on, we aren't going to do [that] anymore. We ain't gonna burn. . . . We put you all to work.[3]

Laboring to Live

The ghetto residents saw that the people the Nazis deported were the very young, the old, the sick, and the weak. At twenty, Blanka Rothschild was old enough to realize that in order to avoid the selections at Lodz, she had to work for her enemies: "[I had a job in] some sort of kitchen. They were feeding for two weeks soup to workers who were essential to their production in [the] ghetto. You see, [the] ghetto had several establishments working for the Germans. In order to stay alive, we were obligated to produce some work."[4]

At eighteen, Lily Margules understood the importance of having a job in the Vilna ghetto: "You could only go out from the ghetto if you had a work permit. And you could only actually survive if you worked because the portions of the Russians [outside the ghetto] are very meager and people were very anxious to work."[5]

Every able-bodied person, including children, became a slave laborer. At seventeen, Dawid Sierakowiak wrote in his diary, "I'll start my work in the saddlery workshop tomorrow. My student career has been suspended, at least for a while. The main thing now is to make an income and survive poverty." A year later Sierakowiak wrote, "All I care is that there is soup in my workshop." The following month he wrote, "We arc not considered humans at all; just cattle for work or slaughter."[6]

At fourteen, Karolina Dresler toiled in a sewing workshop in the Lodz ghetto, making clothes that would be sent to Germany: "They told us to sit in the corner and let us cut circles from a material to make shoulder pads. We were a group, maybe ten children, different ages. There were younger children than me as well. And they ordered us to cut these circles."[7]

Thirteen-year-old Rut Berlinska received a bowl of soup for her work as a dressmaker in Lodz: "We sewed small dresses, hounds-tooth pattern. For two years same cut, same dress. I sewed sleeves, small sleeves with a cuff."[8]

Children who were too young for the workshops took care of household responsibilities while their parents worked. Fifteen-year-old Yitskhok Rudashevski was such a child in Vilna:

> The Jews must live in blocks according to units where they are working. We too must move to the block. . . . My parents work and I have become the "mistress" in the house. I have learned to cook, to wash floors. . . . I have rarely done any cooking until now. It is hard to do everything at the same time.[9]

The Kutno ghetto was established in early 1940, soon after the German occupation of Poland in September 1939. Here, a woman cooks at a makeshift outdoor kitchen as a man wearing a Star of David on his coat looks on.

Working on the Outside

Though Jews were meant to be confined to the ghettos, the Nazis also had work that needed to be done outside of them, and they took Jews to use as slave labor Nineteen-year-old Beno Helmer had to do such work:

> [In] 1942, I got a job . . . outside of the [Krakow] ghetto. I was working for the Germans . . . because I was studying architecture. So they needed some kind of building, the Germans. So they took a forced labor out of the ghetto, so we should work in the construction there. Since I had a so-called background of two days, so (laughing) they made me in charge of it.[10]

At seventeen, David Lieberman had a backbreaking assignment outside the Czestochowa ghetto:

> We were assigned jobs. . . . My job was to work on the Russian cemetery. The Russian soldiers they captured . . . from the war, so they brought them into concentration

Many Jewish men living in ghettos or concentration camps were forced to do hard labor, such as building walls or digging trenches and graves. The men here are being guarded by Nazi soldiers as they dig, circa 1938.

> camp and never gave them any food. They gave them raw potatoes and they died of dysentery, all kinds of diseases. So my job is to work on the cemetery—dig holes. They used to bring truck load of thousands of Russian soldiers.[11]

Some Jews worked as the personal servants of their captors. David Selznick was a young man who worked for the Ghettowache, the Jewish police of the Kovno ghetto. During the liquidation phase—when the Nazis would empty an entire ghetto to be sent to a death camp—German officers took over the police unit, and Selznick was assigned to those officers:

> I and all the other slaves for the Ghettowache were immediately taken away from the ghetto and they built special bungalows, special quarters, upstairs of this school for us to be there and to stay there and not to go back to the ghetto. By then it was a big kitchen with maybe several hundred SS guards, and it required more people to work. And quite a few . . . together with me, and they became permanent laborers, slave laborers, for the Ghettowache. . . . I continued with the same duties of cleaning the toilets, cleaning the rooms, peeling potatoes, peeling beans for the kitchen, and all other manual labor work. In addition to that . . . one of the PX managers . . . had a bicycle, and he constantly instructed me to clean his bicycles.[12]

Jobs outside the ghetto were coveted for one main reason: as Selznick explained, "Every outside work brigade had the opportunity to buy food."[13]

Nineteen-year-old Beno Helmer said of his construction job outside the Krakow ghetto, "What's only good about it was this: they gave us a half a loaf of bread coming home."[14]

Whether inside or outside the ghetto, with so many dying of hunger, any job associated with food meant life. Blanka Rothschild worked in a bakery in the Lodz ghetto for three months. Of that job she said, "That was a life-saving because I could eat some bread in the bakery, and I could take some small pieces home, and my ration card was being used by my family."[15] Later, she worked in the ghetto kitchen. When she lost that job, she noted that it had been "a tragedy because that's where the food was. . . . I was very happy. . . . I was peeling potatoes all day long, and trying to steal some of the peels to take home, because peels meant food."[16]

Leaders of the Imprisoned

Work meant the possibility of living longer. But the number of jobs was limited—supply couldn't meet demand—and the bullets of the Gestapo seemed endless. Who decided who could work? Who chose people for the nicest assignments? Instead of making decisions themselves, the Nazis used a more sinister approach. Thomas Toivi Blatt, twelve when Germany invaded his city of Izbica, Poland, recognized that the Nazis ruled through Jewish leaders:

> The Germans at that time established Jewish Councils, so-called "Judenrat." And through the Judenrat, they were able to execute their orders, so the Judenrat sent people to work in the labor camps and the Judenrat also after a month or so sent new people. The old ones . . . the first ones should be released. So it wasn't an order. Now, everybody, according to the rules . . . was supposed to go for one month to the labor.[17]

Choosing people for work assignments was only one task of the Judenrat. These respected Jewish elders also administered the social service agencies that helped keep the bodies and spirits of the ghetto residents alive. They ran the hospitals, orphanages, soup kitchens, and schools. In addition, the Judenrat served as the liaison between the Jews and the Nazis. Sonia Heidocovsky Zissman explained: "Well, anything the Germans wanted they talked to the Judenrat and they tell them, 'Look. We want so much of so much and we're going to get it.' So, the Judenrat had to go to the Jews, to the rest of them."[18]

The members of the Judenrat were in a difficult situation. They wanted to make life bearable for the Jews, but the Nazis made ruthless demands on them. When the Nazis began deporting ghetto residents to the camps, they

This portrait shows the administrative staff of the Judenrat, or Jewish leadership council, of the Kielce ghetto of Poland. The picture appeared in an album compiled by the Judenrat in 1942.

often made the Judenrat decide who would go and who would stay.

Some of the Jews saw the elders of the Judenrat as men who did their best in impossible circumstances. Sonia Heidocovsky Zissman recognized their dilemma:

> From what I know or remember they were good guys because it was a small, little town and everybody knew everybody. And everybody had brothers, sisters, uncles. . . . So it was different [from] in a big city. We knew each other by name, so I wouldn't say they were working for [the Germans], but there were certain things they had to supply to them or they're going to take out 20 Jews or 50 Jews and kill them if you don't get it.[19]

Others thought the members of the Judenrat abused their power. They thought they kept the best food for themselves, gave more rations to people who paid them something, or put the names of people they disliked on the deportation lists. Blanka Rothschild believed that the leader of the Lodz ghetto, Mordechai Chaim Rumkowski, was not fair:

> Before the war, he was an agent for an orphanage and collected money for the orphans. Since my family was involved in charitable work and donated money to the orphanage, my grandmother decided that I should go to see him and ask him for some help because there was some sort of help. There were . . . small pieces of paper for some food distribution, and I went to see him. . . . And I said to him in Polish, "Panye President," which means Mr. President. At that moment he picked up a cane and wanted to hit me because he resented the

fact that I didn't speak Jewish [Yiddish] to him, which I didn't know.[20]

In her diary, fifteen-year-old Sara Rachela Plagier described the leader of the Lodz Judenrat with mixed feelings:

> Chaim Rumkowski was an absolute monarch. He could banish anyone he wished from the ghetto. He could transfer people from one place to work in another. He could send people to prison. He was all-powerful. Nevertheless, when it came to the Germans, he could do nothing. They could raise their hands or their clubs against him, beat him, kill him. But among us he was the king. We called him by all sorts of titles: "His Excellency the Chairman," "The Eldest of the Jews." And we called him "King."[21]

If anyone disagreed with the decisions of the Judenrat, they would be taking out their frustration and fear on their fellow Jews, rather than the Nazis. By forcing the Judenrat to make these tough decisions, Nazis created division and anger among Jews, making the ghettos an even more difficult place to be than they already were.

Smuggling and Sneaking

No matter how kind or powerful the Judenrat might be, they could not ease the overwhelming complaint of the people in the ghettos: unrelenting hunger. The Nazis controlled the food supply into the ghettos and permitted only starvation rations, usually just bread and potatoes. Often the food was spoiled, and sometimes the rations consisted of nothing more than potato peelings.

Ghetto residents resorted to a desperate measure: smuggling food in from the Aryan side of the city. And

The young people in this portrait helped to smuggle goods in and out of the Warsaw ghetto. Jewish teenagers who looked somewhat Aryan would travel on the Aryan side of Warsaw in order to transport items and information.

the best smugglers were children. Nine-year-old Hanka Ziegler and her brother kept their family alive in the Piotrkow ghetto:

> My father got caught foraging for food and was put in prison. I never saw my father again. . . . My brother Zigmund and I were the breadwinners. He was about 14. We collected all the food. He and I started selling bread and potatoes. We didn't have anything else to sell. And then we started scavenging and begging from non-Jewish people. Being such small children we could get through any hole. We learned how to steal, how to beg. My mother was unable to do anything. She just couldn't cope. We were very hungry. So we went out of the ghetto. We went backwards and forwards. Then the day came when they sealed the ghetto.[22]

Even after the ghettos were sealed, children continued to slip to the Aryan side in search of life-sustaining food. Thirteen-year-old Judith Meisel was able to smuggle food into the Kovno ghetto in Lithuania because she looked Aryan:

> There was a . . . man by the name of Motke. . . . He picked certain children who were blue-eyed, blond, and

> decided we didn't look Jewish, like people thought Jews should look. And he told us that if we are to survive we are to smuggle food into the ghetto. So people gave me some valuables and he opened up a barbed wire with his pliers. He showed how to open up the barbed wire and escape through it from the ghetto and then tell us where we could go and get food. I can remember carrying butter and bread in my underwear to bring back to the ghetto and to going through the sentry and being afraid.[23]

Children, as well as their parents, had good reason to be afraid. Charlene Perlmutter Schiff was caught trying to bring two eggs into the ghetto of Horochow, Poland. The guard yelled at the thirteen-year-old and threatened her, but he let her go. Shortly afterward, she realized how fortunate she was:

> A few days later, one of my best friends . . . snuck out of the ghetto, and she obtained some bread, and as she was trying to get back into the ghetto she was caught and she was murdered. They displayed her body in the ghetto for about a week, and we were forced to march by and look at her. And they didn't allow the burial society to bury her. These were lessons that we learned every day.[24]

The murder of young smugglers was intended to crush the crime. The displaying of the bodies was meant to crush the spirit. In the ghettos, feeding the body was only half the battle for survival. The other half was feeding the spirit.

Chapter 5

Clinging to Hope

When we talk about survival, we often think of things that keep the body going, like food, water, and shelter. But it is equally important to have things that uplift the mind and spirit. Before Hitler's rise to power, the Jews of Europe enjoyed rich cultural lives. Some of the greatest European writers, musicians, and artists were Jewish. When the dark cloud of Nazism weighed down so many, art, including theater, music, and literature, became a hugely important part of helping to lift the spirits of those fighting fascism and anti-Semitism across the continent. Cultural arts also helped Jews find some emotional escape in the midst of a traumatic and terrifying experience.

Finding a Refuge in Art

In 1942, two years after Germany invaded the Netherlands, the Nazis turned a refugee camp in the town of Westerbork into a ghetto-like camp for Jews whom they would eventually send to Auschwitz, a Nazi death camp. To hide the reality of the fate that awaited the Jews of Westerbork, the Nazis permitted them to stage dramas and concerts. Sixteen-year-old William Lowenberg, a Jewish refugee from a small town in Germany, loved the artistic expressions in Westerbork:

> There was a whole community of life. . . . Children would go to school. . . . They had a wonderful orchestra. Then they had opera and theater. Because there was a whole element of German Jews who had come from Berlin mostly, from the stages, intellectual community, the artists who developed in Westerbork an infrastructure of some very beautiful entertainment. For me it was beautiful because I came from a small town and I had never been to opera before in my life. . . . People who were in the camp could go in the evenings after the Germans had gotten their share of it. In Westerbork you could read. . . . In the camp there were some books.[1]

Entertainment, such as what was permitted at Westerbork, was not the norm in the ghettos. After the deportations became regular features of ghetto life, the Nazis no longer felt the need to placate any Jews. Instead, they tried to break their spirits as well as their bodies. They did this by stripping the Jews of everything they valued. Even young children like Inge Auerbacher felt broken:

> When I was 7, I was deported with my parents to the Theresienstadt ghetto in Czechoslovakia. When we arrived, everything was taken from us, except for the clothes we wore and my doll, Marlene. Conditions . . . were harsh. Potatoes were as valuable as diamonds. I was hungry, scared and sick most of the time.[2]

But often, for the sake of their children, parents mustered up the strength and creativity to bring some joy into the darkness. Auerbacher remembered: "For my

Members of the string orchestra at the Westerbork camp in the Netherlands pose with their instruments. Westerbork was known for the vibrant artistic scene that developed despite harrowing conditions.

eighth birthday, my parents gave me a tiny potato cake with a hint of sugar; for my ninth birthday, an outfit sewn from rags for my doll [Marlene]; and for my tenth birthday, a poem written by my mother."[3]

What parents could not provide, children sometimes had to provide on their own. Oskar Rosenfeld, an Austrian Jewish writer who was deported to the Lodz ghetto, published a newspaper for the ghetto and kept a diary of life under Nazi domination. He wrote:

> Toys . . . are things our youngsters must, of course, do without. . . . And so, on their own, they invent toys to replace all the things to delight children everywhere and are unavailable here. The ghetto toy in the summer

> of 1943: Two small slabs of wood [held between the fingers and struck to make sounds]. . . . The streets of the Litzmannstadt [Lodz] ghetto are filled with clicking, drumming, banging. . . . Barefoot boys scurry past you, performing their music right under your nose, with great earnestness.[4]

Illegal Education

One way the Nazis tried to crush people's spirits was to stifle any kind of learning. Emanuel Tanay recalled that in Miechow, "There was no official school. I did go, I had a teacher, but that was illegal. And in fact it was punishable by death."[5]

Despite the risk, Jewish adults organized many lessons for their children. Ephraim Dekel described the school in the ghetto of Shavli, Lithuania:

> My job was to manage the ghetto school. It was a unique school. Our oppressors had forbidden us to educate our children. Therefore we had established an undercover school: We have arranged the children in small classes and distributed them in rooms all over the ghetto. . . . Class after class, our children sneaked into their school. They crowded the rooms and for two hours listened to lessons from their teachers. Then they went out secretly to make room for a second class. They came to school hungry and naked, and only once a week, on Friday after taking a hot bath, their teachers could also provide them with a slice of bread with some jelly.[6]

The children came to the forbidden schools not only for the bread, but because learning kept their spirits strong. Yitskhok Rudashevski, thirteen when he was deported to the Vilna ghetto, wrote in his diary:

Thousands of children were transferred to the Kovno ghetto in Lithuania when it was created in 1941. Formal education was banned in 1942, but children continued to attend secret schools.

> After long hesitation and long reflection I decided to make use of every moment. I need to study; I still have suitable conditions, so I must not interrupt my studies. My determination to study has developed into something like defiance of the present which hates to study, loves to work, to drudge. No, I decided. I shall live with tomorrow, not with today. And if for every hundred ghetto children my age [only] ten can study, I must take advantage of this. Studying has become more precious to me than before.[7]

Going to school, even in such difficult conditions, helped make life in the ghettos feel a little more normal, and children valued the experience of learning deeply.

Keeping Religion Alive

Synagogues had been closed and many religious practices outlawed. But ghetto residents found ways to observe their faith. Avraham Golub described the observance of Purim, a normally joyous festival commemorating a great deliverance of the Jewish people, in the Kovno ghetto:

"Here in the ghetto we are celebrating Purim in a new style. None other than our children [are] celebrating Purim with all their innocence and enthusiasm. . . . The children have been preparing the Purim festivities for many weeks. They have been learning the Purim songs, the dances, the games. . . . The children have been telling their parents all about their Purim preparations, and the parents—if there are any parents left alive—let themselves be drawn in by the festive atmosphere."[8]

Voices Raised in Song

Festivities could not only draw people in but could lift them above their desperate circumstances. In the Theresienstadt ghetto in Czechoslovakia, for a very short time, music helped transport residents out of their crowded quarters back to their prewar lives. Twelve-year-old Fritzie Weiss Fritzshall was grateful for the music: "I thought I am back in Prague in a concert scene. . . . You forget where you are . . . those two years. . . . You hear the music, you hear the concerts, you hear the opera . . . and you were back in the National Theater hearing the opera."[9]

A rabbi reads the Talmud during Sabbath services in 1941. Jewish religious services were banned in most ghettos, so Jews prayed and held ceremonies in secret.

The Theresienstadt ghetto (also called Terezin) was different from most. Half ghetto, half concentration camp, it was a Nazi showplace. The Gestapo kept it a little cleaner and a little less crowded than most other ghettos. When the Nazis wanted the world to believe they treated Jews kindly, they showed them Theresienstadt, which they called a "model camp."

Despite the charade, the ghetto remained a dismal place. The Gestapo was just as brutal, and life remained terribly insecure, but there were also many intellectuals and artists living there. One in particular saw the need to lift people's spirits: Edgar Krasa, who volunteered in 1941

An image of Rafael Schächter is displayed at a 2013 mass in Prague in memory of Schächter and other musicians who died in the Terezin concentration camp.

to go to Theresienstadt as a cook to keep his parents from being deported to Poland, was energized when the famous conductor Rafael Schächter came to the camp at the end of November 1941:

> He recognized immediately upon his arrival that the prison mentality can sink into the people's mind. That when he came, when the gates were still closed, and he got everybody together and encouraged them to sing. And most of the songs were Czech popular songs, which most of people knew. And it had a tremendous impact on everybody, not just during the time you were singing. . . . Others who were not singing were sitting there and listening, to the point that not just that hour, hour and a half, you forgot every—that the reality of your actual circumstances, but you took with you a little bit of—like a care package, a spiritual care package to help you carry on . . . until the next time when we sing.[10]

Krasa was twenty-one when Schächter came to Theresienstadt. He welcomed the chance to sing with him:

> I was in the crowd of all the others who went to sing with him, whom he encouraged to sing. . . . [During] the last three or four months in Prague [before being deported to the ghetto] . . . the Jewish communities had free evenings. . . . I joined a barbershop quartet. . . . As a bass. . . . I don't think we were singing for money, we were singing I think only for pleasure. And so I liked singing, and so I definitely volunteered to participate.[11]

Krasa was not the only volunteer. Schächter put together a choir of one hundred fifty voices. They practiced at night, so their cultural activity did not disturb or anger the Nazis. Eventually, they held performances, and many of the Nazi guards attended. Krasa recalled:

Prisoners walk through the gate of the Theresienstadt concentration camp. Theresienstadt was originally built as a temporary transit camp for Czech Jews. It later became something between a ghetto and a labor camp. The sign above the gate is translated as "Work Sets You Free."

ARBEIT MACHT FREI

> Most evenings I spent singing with Schachter. . . . We had almost every night the rehearsal. . . . After June '42, when people could move freely, he assembled the men and the women together in the basement of the military headquarters near—on the right of the church. . . . And that was during the day, a carpenter shop, and at night we put up some boards . . . and the choir stood there and was singing and rehearsing. As soon as we could get together, he came up.[12]

Krasa noted that the choir had very little with which to work in Theresienstadt:

> He had one score of *The Bartered Bride*, as a very popular Czech opera, and started to study with us. The singers had nothing to look at. There was no written music, there were no way of copying, and no time to copy, and not enough qualified people to copy music. So we learned by rote [memorizing and repeating]. . . . There was a harmonium. . . . [A work detail] discovered somewhere in the room an old harmonium. So one night they, when it was dark, no moon, they brought the harmonium to that basement. And first . . . Schachter was playing the harmonium, and then they found a piano without legs, and also brought it in, and the carpenters made some legs. Until they made the legs and fastened them, the piano was standing on three crates.[13]

The conductor took what little he had and brought some life to the otherwise hopeless ghetto residents:

> Schachter was a loveable, pleasant person, until he sat behind the piano, then he became a tyrant. You were not allowed to look at the guy next to you, or even at the girl next to you. You were not allowed to whisper. You had to focus on his eyes, because he was conducting

> with his eyes— the hands on the keys, and his eyes were directing the music. And if he noticed . . . you're not attentive—once, he yelled at you, the second time he threw you out. . . . And nobody minded it, everybody wanted to be part of it.[14]

Keeping everyone's spirits up may have been hard for Schächter. On two occasions, the deportation trains took nearly everyone in his choir, and he had to start over. In January 1943, the transports slowed. Hoping that he could maintain a choir, Schächter decided on a daring idea: he would train everyone who would volunteer to perform Verdi's *Requiem*.

Verdi's *Requiem* was a collection of songs for a funeral. But Schächter was not thinking of death. He was thinking of the words of some of the songs. "Dies Irae" spoke of God's anger, and "Libera Me" was a prayer for freedom. Schächter wanted to tell his Nazi captors that God would pour out His wrath on them. But not everyone thought singing the *Requiem* was wise. Krasa recalled:

> There was a huge uproar when he came up with that idea. All the scholars and professors, . . . and the Council of Elders [the Judenrat], they all protested for different reasons. The scholars and the rabbis: Why would you, as Jews in a Jewish ghetto, perform a Catholic mass for the dead, when there are comparable works on Jewish themes? . . . He didn't say it openly because it was dangerous to say, but I know that his mind was on . . . wanting to be able to sing to the Germans in Latin what he couldn't tell them in German to their face. Like the *Dies Irae*—the Day of Wrath. That in his [God's] book, the names of all the sinners are inscribed, and none will escape the punishment. . . . The Council of Elders

> thought, if the Germans find out the intentions behind this performance, that will really be dangerous for the singers and for him, and maybe even implications for the rest of the population.[15]

In the end, Schächter won. During the next two years, the choir performed the music sixteen times. It gave hope to those who sang and those who heard it. Fourteen-year-old Hana Fuchs Krasa was stirred as she listened:

> I at least knew what they are singing about because my friend told me. She was singing for us. . . . I took Latin in school, . . . so I knew what "libera" may mean ["free"] even if I didn't understand every word, and couldn't translate it for anybody. . . . It was very powerful. . . . My friend told me what the meaning is:
>
> To tell them [the Nazis] that they will suffer. In the end, truth will win somehow, and we wanted to believe that.[16]

Loneliness and Silence

Only one ghetto had the benefit of Schächter's music. In most, singing was rare. How did children in these songless cities feed their spirits? Some composed their own songs and poems to keep hope alive. Sixteen-year-old Miriam Goldberg continued to dream amidst the despair of the Lodz ghetto. She wrote:

> I sit next to a table with a broken glass
> And look at a street full of mud.
> I dream that somewhere is a land full of sun,
> Somewhere, a field of golden wheat.[17]

Often, however, the children's writings expressed more despair than hope. One young girl confided in her diary:

> Beautiful, sunny day today. When the sun shines, my mood is lighter. How sad life is. When we look at the fence separating us from the rest of the world, our souls, like birds in a cage, yearn to be free. Longing breaks my heart, visions of the past come to me. Will I ever live in better times?[19]

The writer, like 1.5 million other children, probably did not live to see better times.

Chapter 6

From Ghettos to Death Camps

As one step in the path to Hitler's final solution, the ghettos were never meant to be permanent. They were holding spaces, meant to keep Jews away from the rest of the populace until they could be systematically murdered, either in the death camps or in the ghettos themselves. Yet the people living in them didn't know that—they thought that the ghettos were simply their new home. It was a difficult, cramped, unhappy life, but it was a life. In 1942, however, the death camps were in full operation, and in the summer of that year the Nazis began systematically taking people out of the ghettos and shipping them to the killing centers.

The Path to the Death Camps

The process of moving people to the death camps was different in each ghetto, depending on the size of the ghetto and the capacity of the particular death camp at that time. For example, the ghettos in and around Krakow were emptied in a series of deportations from mid-1942 to December 1943. Large-scale thinning of the Warsaw ghetto began in the summer of 1942 and ended in May 1943 after an uprising. Some of the smaller ghettos were emptied in a matter of weeks or months. In Lodz, tens of thousands were killed in 1942. However, the mass deportations stopped for two years, resuming in the summer of 1944, because Germany was in desperate need of workers for its armaments factories and needed to keep some Jews alive in order to keep them as a source of free labor.

The large ghettos were reduced gradually, in a series of *Aktionen*, or roundups, of thousands of people at a time. Thomas Toivi Blatt, who was eventually deported to, but survived, the death camp of Sobibor, escaped the first transports from the Izbica ghetto:

> As the time progressed, it was worse and worse. We heard about beating. We heard about torture, and people refused to go [when the Germans ordered them to appear for work]. In that time the first so-called "Aktions" happened. "Aktion" is a roundup. It started with roundups to the labor camps. They would come in the morning and told the Jewish Council to deliver 500 men or 200 men. If the Jewish Council wasn't able to deliver through their own police, [the Nazis] started indiscriminate to go from house to house, beat, shot. . . . And they . . . simply caught people on the streets 'til they get the amount of 500 people and they took them away.[1]

For some time, the residents did not know where the transports were going. Abraham Malnik was fifteen when the deportations began in Kovno:

> It was the 28th of October in 1942, they sent out some fliers that next day all the people should get together

At a train station in Poland, Nazi officers corral anxious Jews in preparation for sending them to concentration camps.

> and they should assemble themselves in a place called the Democracy Place. . . . In the evening there were accumulated about 10,000 people in that small compound. . . . What our destination [was] we still didn't know. We thought that maybe they're gonna give us other work. We never thought they're gonna kill us. After all, 10,000 people. But the Germans had their own plans.[2]

The Nazis marched all ten thousand people to the nearby Ninth Fort and shot them there. Abraham was one of only three people to escape. Two years later, when the Kovno ghetto was liquidated, Abraham was sent to the first of five concentration camps, all of which he survived.

Lies and "Resettlement"

The people did not know where they were going because the Nazis lied to them. To keep them calm, the Germans told them they were going to be resettled, as the Nazis called it, in a better place. They had used the same tactic earlier, when they banished the Jews of Germany and Austria to the ghettos of the east. One resident of the Kovno ghetto, whose job was to sort through the possessions of the Jews who were to be killed, saw the deception close up:

> They start bringing to the railroad station . . . boxcars with the Jews from Austria and Germany. They called that [by a word that meant] "take them from one place and put them into another place" in German. And this train came with cars loaded with pianos, with furniture, with all kinds of luxury items, to make believe to those people—because . . . when they took [them] out from Germany or from Austria Jews to send them to their . . . graves . . . they had to handle it in a certain way.

The liquidation of the Kovno ghetto began three weeks before Soviet soldiers liberated the Lithuanian city. After the ghetto was liquidated, Nazi troops razed the buildings and burned it to the ground.

> They tried to convince them that they are being taken to another place.[3]

The Nazis took great pains to keep up the charade. The Kovno ghetto worker watched but was threatened with a bullet to his head if he spoke:

> A German would say . . . "Give me your packs. . . . You have to walk a few kilometers. Please give us your packages because it's going to be very burdensome and we are placing these packages in the trucks and we are going to deliver them. And make sure to describe your names on the packages so we are going to know how to return them to you."[4]

Young Yitskhok Rudashevski watched families who thought they were being resettled from the Vilna ghetto to a better place:

> Sunday at three o'clock the streets in the ghetto were closed off. A group of three hundred of the Jews . . . have left for Kovno with a large transport of provincial Jews that arrived at the railway station. As I stood at the gate I saw how they were packing their things. Gaily and in high spirits they went to the train.[5]

But the terrible truth could not be hidden for long. Rumors seeped into the ghetto, and people began to suspect the unbelievable. Emanuel Tanay's parents debated what might happen:

> My mother, in contrast to my father, was sort of obsessed with a notion that something terrible is happening. . . . She was full of fear and she talked to people she knew. Polish people. My father didn't quite believe it. He had more of a notion that, these were all rumors. . . . Germans are civilized people. I mean, here there are

> excesses because of some individual situations. So he was much more given to the idea that things will work out whereas my mother was full of anxiety.[6]

Witnesses who escaped the scenes of slaughter reported back to the ghetto what they had seen. The day after Yitskhok waved farewell to happy Jews, he wrote in his diary: "Today the terrible news reached us: eighty-five railroad cars of Jews, around five thousand persons, were not taken to Kovno as promised but transported by train to Ponar where they were shot to death."[7] The next day, he wrote:

> We now know all the horrible details. . . . Like wild animals before dying, the people began in mortal despair to break the railroad cars. They broke the little windows reinforced by strong wire. Hundreds were shot to death while running away.
>
> The railroad line over a great distance is covered with corpses.[8]

Normalization of Brutality

The first news of mass slaughter may have shocked the ghetto residents, but eventually the murders became an unavoidable fact of life. When fifteen-year-old Abraham Malnik narrowly escaped the massacre at Kovno, he "went back to the ghetto. . . . And the life 'became normal.'"[9] Fourteen-year-old Emanuel Tanay lived through several Aktionen at Miechow:

> A number of times [our family was] separated. . . . The ghetto, I am assuming, at its height was six thousand people in our town. Then there would be a liquidation and it would be smaller and smaller and smaller. But

For the most part, ghetto residents didn't know where they were being sent on the trains. Here, a woman waves from a train headed toward a concentration camp in 1940.

> when they did have one of those liquidations, children, women, were the ones who were first deported. So, when you found out that that was happening, my parents would either hide me or send me someplace or my sister. . . . Then we will come back to the ghetto. Because, you know, they would liquidate the ghetto, then Jews would come back, and things would go back to normal. Maybe for six months or . . . so on. So there were a number of such separations.[10]

Between the actions, normal life for children consisted of just trying to stay alive. Amalie Petranker Salsitz, nineteen when she was closed inside the Krakow ghetto, explained:

> The ghetto was life, in between the killings, going on semi-normal. We tried. We hoped this [each *Aktion*] is the end, especially when Roosevelt [and the United States] entered the war. We thought we will be saved. Everybody just tried to live another day with the hope that they would survive.[11]

Because the Nazis could not kill everyone at once, they first took the "unproductive" people. Salsitz described the system:

> They will have killings in the ghetto. You know, they assigned the Jews, classified the Jews, just to find excuse for each killing which they call an aktion. First were the children. Then were all the old people. Then were people who were sick, people who couldn't work, so was A, B, C classification.[12]

The Plight of Children

The young children were obviously of no use to the Nazis. At sixteen, Sara Rachela Plagier escaped a deportation of children from the Lodz ghetto. She wrote of the scene in her diary:

> I saw two wagons full of little children drive past the open gate. Many of the children were dressed in their holiday best, the little girls with colored ribbons in their hair. In spite of the soldiers in their midst, the children were shrieking at the top of their lungs. They were calling out for their mothers.[13]

But their parents could not help them. Brigitte Friedmann Altman, age twenty, watched a roundup of children in the last days of the Kovno ghetto:

> At that time [March 1944] there were very few children left in the ghetto. Frantically, the grandmother had put

During the Warsaw Ghetto Uprising in spring 1943, children were taken from their parents and deported to the Treblinka and Sobibór camps on livestock wagons

> the . . . little girl into the bed . . . and had heaped all the blankets and quilts . . . so it would look that it was just a made up bed. . . . One of the soldiers or officers confronts me and wants to know why I'm not at my workplace. Fortunately I was dressed. I showed him my work permit, but . . . I was stunned, petrified, and my heart was racing. . . . He . . . spoke to me sternly, then shoved me away . . . and started tearing up the room. I think all three did that, they tore up the room, and it didn't take them any time to tear apart the bed clothes, to come upon the little girl. . . . When they made sure there was nobody else hiding and nothing else was to be found, they dragged her out, towards this truck. And the grandmother . . . ran, ran after them . . . fell down . . . fell on her knees, begged, pleaded, cried, wailed, followed, followed them out to the truck, to the curb and one of the soldiers either used his gun or a club and hit her and she fell to the ground, she fell down in the street. The truck took off and she was left behind. They took the little girl, there were other children on the truck.[14]

No More Pretending

By 1943, all pretense was gone. The Nazis unleashed their full brutality on their helpless victims. Deportations began to occur more frequently. Eight-year-old Thomas Buergenthal remembered a deportation from the Kielce ghetto: "One morning we were awakened with screaming and shooting outside—orders in German: 'Everybody out!' And whoever wasn't to be out would be shot, and apparently a lot of older people, others who couldn't move, were shot."[15]

The fact that the ghettos were intended for death no longer needed to be hidden. Amalie Petranker Salsitz knew when the change from pretense to open action took place in Krakow: "One day we saw through the window [an] aktion. . . . There was no secret. Openly, in the ghetto they digged ditches and they shot on the spot so everybody had seen it. . . . They just had done it first on the Jewish cemetery, but then when there's no room anymore, they had done it in the ghetto."[16]

Children saw their parents gunned down mercilessly. Eve Wagszul Rich lost her father in the Kowol ghetto:

> We knew that sooner or later they're going to either kill us or take us to labor camps, the younger people. . . . One night that I remember so well, we were told to leave the house. For some reason my father wouldn't leave the house. [The Germans] broke down the door. The doors were locked. They came in. My father has a talis [prayer shawl] on. He prayed. And they killed him in front of my eyes.[17]

Older children took responsibility for their elderly relatives. Henny Fletcher Aronson, although at twenty years of age was not particularly muscular, found the strength to lift and carry her mother-in-law, who could not care for herself:

> Suddenly the loud speaker started screaming: All the people and children out. And my mother-in-law . . . was a semi-invalid [unable to walk], a wonderful woman, an exceptional lady. . . . She was a fabulous cook . . . a pharmacist by education, a wonderful lady. We didn't know what to do. We knew she could not walk, so I looked at my brother-in-law, and he looked at me, and I said, "Let's hide her someplace." But before we had a

chance to do anything, they just broke into the room . . . and they said out to her from bed. And I stood in front of her and I said, "She can't go, walk." So they gave me a slap. "She can't walk? So you carry her." So I said to Misha, my brother-in-law, "Let's put something on her." She was wearing a nightgown. . . . They wouldn't let us do anything. They made my brother-in-law grab her by the shoulders, and I had to grab her by the foot. I tried to pull down her dress. . . . And we carried her out. And the street was a nightmare because all you could see were young people carrying these old people like animals. And we carried her to the place where the buses were stationed. And [the German] told my brother-in-law . . . to stay, and I'm the one who should

Death Camps in Poland

Many of the most infamous Nazi death camps were located in Poland, both because of the large Jewish population there and because it was removed from the rest of Germany. Although Nazis now controlled the German government, they couldn't afford for citizens to become suspicious or change their minds about having Nazis in power. Death camps were facilities designed to kill massive numbers of people all at once using poisonous gases, though inhabitants of concentration camps were also used as slave labor or simply shot as well. One of the most famous death camps is Auschwitz. Originally built to house Polish political prisoners, it became a major killing center during World War II, and it is thought that over one million people died there.

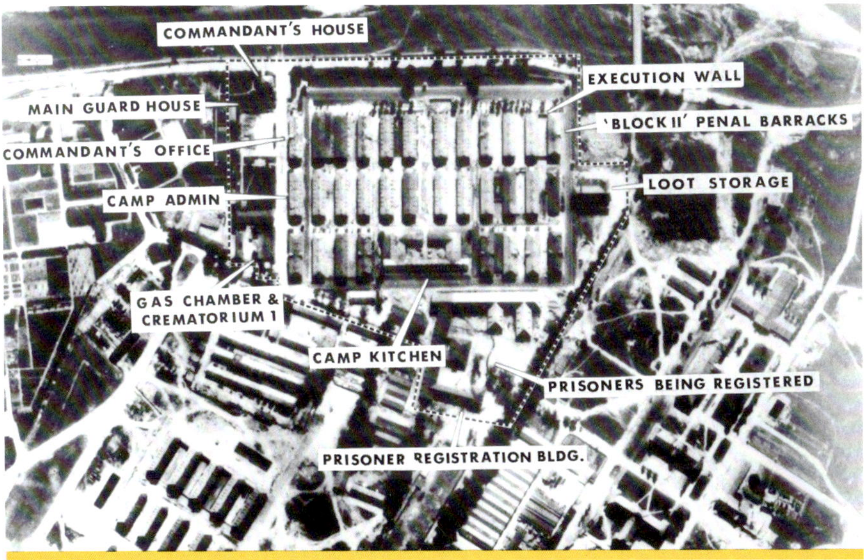

Using contemporary photo analysis on images taken during reconnaissance missions in World War II, analysts have been able to produce an image of the Birkenau extermination facility at Auschwitz.

> carry her out. Now, she was a frail woman. I must have picked her up, and I walked up on the bus, and I figured that's the end of me too. . . . There was no seat, so I had to put her in the aisle, and I covered her up. They looked around to find a seat for me. So, they pushed me down the stairs and said, "You get out of there."[18]

The absence of a seat kept Aronson in the Kovno ghetto while her mother-in-law was murdered.

The Ceaseless Selections

In all the Aktionen before the final liquidation of each ghetto, the residents never knew who would be taken and who would be spared. But at age fifteen, Abraham Malnik began to figure out how the selection process worked at Kovno:

> We all got up in the morning . . . 6 in the morning, and families, with . . . children and babies, everybody assembled themselves. 7 o'clock exactly . . . we were surrounded by the Lithuanian police. . . . We all stayed in columns. And German officers, they were there . . . and they start sorting us. Right and left. We didn't have at that time an idea what's all about it. But we felt that something is wrong because all the older people and the sick ones were going one side and the one who could still work was going on the other side. When it came to us, we were standing in line together—my father, my mother and myself. And my grandmother and my aunt, they were elderly. And because of them, he put us all in the bad side. . . . My mother got very scared and she told my father, "Maybe you can run away. Get out."[19]

Abraham Malnik and his parents managed to dodge this particular selection, but during the sorting process, getting out of the lines usually meant being shot. David Lieberman, seventeen in 1942, could not figure out which line he wanted to join during an *Aktion* in the Czestochowa ghetto:

> A chief of the Gestapo . . . came with his cronies and stood in a certain block. . . . And everybody was passing by in front of him, and he decided which way [for you] to go. Left and right. I didn't know which way was good. Left or right. . . . And this was going on, I think, for a week. Every block, every little district. Then it came to us, finally came to our section. . . . They were shooting and killing.[20]

Fortunately for Lieberman, he got in the good line.

Sorting was the first step in the liquidations. The next step was either being marched to the place of execution or boarding the trains to the death camps. Cecilie Klein-Pollack was deported from the Hungarian city of Huszt. The Nazis took over this area in 1944 and quickly set up ghettos to organize the Jews for transit directly to the death camps. Usually, within a matter of weeks they were shipped out. Cecilie was nineteen when the Nazis liquidated the hastily erected ghetto of Huszt:

> They told us the day before that we can pack one small suitcase and we should be ready to leave the ghetto. When we came to [the gathering place] they started to search us again. The SS was there also, and every woman . . . and every girl had to undress, naked, and we were searched internally for valuables. My mother was a very religious person, and all I could think of was how terrible this is for my mother to go through . . . such a terrible ordeal.
>
> When we were finished, my mother took the baby from my sister . . . and she had a bottle of milk for the child. And the SS grabbed the bottle of milk and said, "Let's see, you cow, what you have there."
>
> My mother pleaded, "Please, this is, the child needs the milk. Please don't take the milk from, from my grandson."
>
> He started to beat her with a horsewhip. And when I saw that she was being beaten, so I screamed. So at least I got away the attention from my mother. So my mother ran into the . . . trains. . . . And he started to beat me with that whip. And finally, I was able to run away also, and we were finally in the cattle train.[21]

Parents and children tried to stay together through the grueling ordeal. Nineteen-year-old Abraham Lewent and his father were able to leave the Warsaw ghetto on the same deportation train:

> One day in the morning the factory didn't open up. Everybody has to be outside in the street. You are not allowed to go up anymore in the apartments you lived. Everybody has to be outside. Around 10 o'clock . . . trucks [came] and start loading up all the goods from the houses, from the apartments. . . . Around 12 or 1 o'clock in the afternoon, they tell us to get ready, we gonna walk. . . . So my father and me, my father's friend and his friend, we all stick together and we walked. That means we walked about—I'll say—8 or 10 miles towards the place—the Umschlag place, the famous Umschlag place—to get on trains and take us someplace. We don't know where. . . .
>
> We carried the suitcases. Only what you are able to carry. That's the time the Polish people came and said, "Leave it here on the street because you have no use for this anymore." Like vultures, and if somebody couldn't carry anymore, they left it and you see them running and grab it.
>
> We went to that Umschlagplatz. We were sitting three days over there without water, without anything for 3 days, and it was hot. The third day they gave us water and they said, "We're gonna leave." And where we're going we don't know. They put us on trains. I was together with my father. . . . And they took us to Majdanek [a work camp and annihilation camp].[22]

Abraham survived Majdanek and seven other camps.

Rescuing the Youngest Prisoners

At some point, most adults realized the Nazis were planning to kill everyone in the ghetto. They clung to the hope that Germany would be defeated before the Nazis could carry out their plans. Unable to save themselves, the adults tried to protect their children. Sol Lurie's father hid the twelve-year-old and four of his cousins when the Nazis made selections in the Kovno ghetto:

> They were taking all the children away from the parents and my father [was] where the stables were, with the horses, we used to have a cellar there, so he took me and my cousin[s] . . . and he put us in that cellar and he put wheat over the . . . trap of the cellar so he figured the Germans weren't going to find us.[23]

But the Germans did find them:

> My cousin, she had asthma and from the wheat, it started to affect her. She couldn't breathe. So . . . she lifted up the cover, and the wheat was starting to fall inside. And then she was trying to close it up, and the wheat must have gotten stuck on the hole there. And when the Germans came into the stable to see if anybody was hiding there in the straw, the wheat seeping into the hole. They opened it up and they found us. . . . I started to run and I jumped into . . . one of the bins there where they put the horse feed . . . and I covered myself with straw.[24]

The Nazis killed all four cousins and came after Sol. He escaped only by lowering himself into a hole of an outhouse and staying there until dark.

Seventeen-year-old Jakub Lapides had no parents to hide him. His instincts saved him from a Nazi deportation of children from the Lodz ghetto:

> One day they announced in our orphanage that we will travel to a different place, and we were told "Take

Prisoners at Auschwitz were given specific clothing to wear, and their heads were shaved as a precaution against lice. These images show mugshots of young boys imprisoned at Auschwitz circa 1940.

everything you can." We went out to wait for the trucks to take us. And then my brother Moshe said to me and Miriam, my sister: "Let's hide in the cemetery." We went and hid there among the gravestones. We saw people bringing huge pots with soup. We were very hungry, and Moshe started to go back. And we followed him to the food line. We hadn't gotten the soup yet, and the trucks arrived and I said, "Let's go back to the cemetery." I ran back. But not Moshe, and not Miriam; they did not come back. They were taken on the trucks [to the death camp].[25]

Fourteen-year-old Chaim Kozienicki did not expect to escape the trains during the *Gehsperre Aktion* of September 1942. This was a weeklong series of deportations from Lodz. Twelve thousand Jews—mainly the sick, the old, and the children—were transported to the Chelmno death camp. Chaim, however, was not among them:

> The selections went from house to house. We had no chance to avoid the deportation. We decided to take everything from our garden and eat it all; the last meal, the last supper. Mother cooked a huge pot of soup. We sat down and started to eat. All around our hut there was yelling and shooting and barking of the dogs. It was all mixed up but we were so invested in eating. We were in an ecstasy of eating. We ate bowl after bowl. When we were ready, we got up to go. Then Father said, "They will take us anyway. Let them come and take us. We don't have to come out." Apparently they looked through the two windows across the hut and did not see us inside, and they left. This was the miracle that happened to us.[26]

The miracle was only a short delay. Less than two years later, in August 1944, the Lodz ghetto was completely liquidated. It was the last ghetto to remain. At that time, no one escaped.

Chapter 7

Liquidation in Full

Thousands and thousands of Jews had already died, either through the hardship and violence of the ghettos or after being moved to death camps, but thousands still remained in the ghettos. On June 11, 1943, Nazi soldiers were ordered to completely liquidate Polish ghettos. Ten days later, the Nazis issued an order to liquidate the ghettos in the Soviet territory as well. Liquidation meant ridding the ghettos of all left living there as quickly as possible. Jews who could work were sent to the labor camps, while others were simply murdered. The ghettos themselves were destroyed. Occasionally, these destroyed ghettos made convenient hiding spots for people on the run or who had managed to stay hidden, but the majority of the ghettos' inhabitants were long gone by then, with no hope of escaping.

Execution and Expulsion

Some of the Jews were massacred at already-bloody execution sites a short distance from the ghetto. Fifteen-year-old Abraham Malnik and his parents lived through an execution outside Kovno because his father begged for mercy and the SS officers relented:

> They had taken out the Jewish and Russian prisoners to Ninth Fort, and they dug trenches. And then they put machine guns. And then they're . . . gonna kill us and bury us. . . . The people were crying. They were separating children from old people.
>
> . . . They . . . were put in bunkers . . . told [they were going to be] stripped until the underwear. And they walked out a hundred at a time. They were machine gunned for three days, and then they covered them up with dirt. They took tractors and ran over the graves in order to squeeze out the last breath.
>
> And when the front [the Soviet army] came closer and the Germans did not want to leave no evidence, they undug the graves and they found mother with children hugged together by dying and with parents, grandmothers. They saw people together. And they burned them all. . . . Wasn't far from the ghetto. . . . From 10,000, just myself, my mother was survived, and my father. And the rest went in [the pit].[1]

Many of the ghetto residents were taken to one of the six death camps. Aaron Elster went from the ghetto in Sokolow, Poland, to Treblinka:

> I am ten years old. In September the German Gestapo and the Ukrainian soldiers plus the Polish police invade the ghetto and start the final liquidation of the Jewish people that are left in the ghetto. We are hiding. My family and neighbors are hiding inside a double wall. It is very scary. I can't stop thinking of death and the pain, the pain that comes with death. They find us quickly and rip open the wall. The SS start shooting into our

After the Warsaw Ghetto Uprising in the spring of 1943, the entire ghetto was destroyed by German soldiers, and surviving ghetto residents were sent to concentration and extermination camps.

hiding place. People are lying around me, bleeding and dying. I know these people; they are not bad people. They have done nothing wrong. They are like me, just like me. We are dragged out of our hiding place. They scream at us, "Out, you dirty Jews!"

We run out of our hiding place into the street. My mother is pulled out of line. My six-year-old sister and me

are with my father. Anyone that's near a guard gets hit with a whip. I am terrified. I'm too scared to even look up. I cannot control my fears and my whole body starts to shake, but I don't cry. I guess I think that if I don't look up in their faces they won't see me. Everywhere I look, people are screaming and being shot. People are being dragged out of their houses, beaten, clubbed, and chased to the back of their homes where they are shot and thrown into a mass grave. The rest are chased up to the main marketplace in the middle of town, but one of the older ladies in our building can't keep up with the rest. So when she falls down on the way to the marketplace, the Gestapo guards don't help her back up. They just kick her until she dies and then they just walked away. The people that are left are pushed and shoved into a line, and then marched to the train that will take them to Treblinka.[2]

Sending Children to Safety

Some of the ghetto residents had connections on the "Aryan" side of the city. Emanuel Tanay's mother was able to use her connections to get her son out of Miechow:

> My mother was full of anxiety and she . . . arranged with some woman that she knew who had . . . a bakery on the Polish side. And my mother could leave the ghetto . . . she had the permit to do so. She talked to [the non-Jewish Polish woman] and through her, she

Jewish and Polish prisoners stand facing the wall in a torture chamber near the Warsaw ghetto in 1942. The man on the far right with the swastika on his arm is a member of the Gestapo, charged with guarding the prisoners.

> arranged for, a man who was in the monastery named Gadomski to come and pick me up and take me to that monastery . . . near Krakow. And that happened really by sheer coincidence [to be] that very night when the final liquidation of the ghetto has occurred. So when I was sleeping in the home of that woman to be picked up next morning, we discovered that the ghetto was surrounded and was liquidated. And I didn't really know what happened to my family, but I was taken by that man . . . to Krakow. And then we went to the monastery and he introduced me to the Opat [Abbot], the head of the monastery, whom he did not tell that I was a Jew.[3]

At times, Gentiles rescued Jewish children. The penalty for hiding a Jew was death. Still, some risked their lives to help the children. Irena Sendlerowa was a young Pole who forged documents, found Poles willing to adopt Jewish children, and took the children to those homes:

> We were given "passes" allowing entry to the Warsaw ghetto as functionaries of the Urban Sanitation Works [healthcare workers]. . . . It soon proved imperative to get children out on the so-called Aryan side since inside the ghetto . . . was hell. We reached homes to say we could rescue children and lead them outside the ghetto walls.[4]

Naturally, parents were torn between keeping their children with them and letting them go, often with strangers. They had heard so many lies, seen so much death. How could they know that sending their children away would really keep them safe? Sendlerowa understood their dilemma:

> The basic question which then arose was: What guarantee could we give? We had to admit honestly that

> we could give no guarantee since we did not even know whether we would succeed in leaving the ghetto today.
>
> That was when we witnessed infernal scenes. Father agreed but mother didn't. Grandmother cuddled the child most tenderly and, weeping bitterly, said, "I won't give away my grandchild at any price."
>
> We sometimes had to leave such unfortunate families without taking their children from them. I went there the next day to see what the whole building had come to and often found that everyone had been taken to the . . . railway siding for transport to death camps.[5]

Attempts at Resistance

The situation for all ghetto residents was grim. Overwhelming force closed off all escape. Still, in at least sixty ghettos, people resisted. They knew they could not overpower their oppressors; their only hope was that some could make it out of the ghetto. If they could escape, they might be able to survive until the war ended. In the forests near some of the smaller ghettos, especially those in the Soviet Union, partisans were hiding. These were anti-Nazi groups, and they were sabotaging Nazi operations.

The Jews in some of the ghettos formed secret groups that plotted ways to rebel. Eighteen-year-old Lily Margules was involved in one of the first ghetto revolts, in Lachwa, in 1942:

> We started hearing that they are going to kill the Jews. . . . And they said to my father that, "I think it's going to happen in the next few days." So . . . they started talking about burning everything, like all the things we have, we should burn. Nobody should have it. Not the Belorus, not the Germans, should get nothing that we

Leah Hammerstein Silverstein (*second from right*) and other surviving members of the Jewish underground in Poland pose above the ruins of the bunker that was formerly their headquarters in the Warsaw ghetto, circa summer 1945.

have. We started putting gasoline when we knew that the next day we're going to get killed. . . .

I went out, I remember, very early in the morning. And I saw the Germans pulling up with guns, with all kinds of things . . . and they were pointing at the ghetto.

> My father was running out of the house and I didn't know what he said. "You wait here. Don't go anyplace. We have to be together now." And they started burning. It wasn't just my father; it was lots of people. . . . They burned everything. . . .
>
> And my father said like that, "Let's run!" Before we were running, I was near water. The water was death. They called the water "death," like "smierc" in Polish. And I saw the Germans. They were fighting with the Jews with knives and with ax. And there was one man . . . and he was holding an ax on a German over the head in the water, and the Germans killed him right away.[6]

Florence Gittelman Eisen was fourteen when Lachwa revolted. Her father was one of the six hundred Jews who escaped the ghetto. Florence was sick, and some of the partisans did not want her to come with them; she would slow them down:

> The house was on fire. I crawled out . . . and I lay down there to die. All by myself. All of a sudden, I open my eyes. I see my father. He was asking, he was asking around if anybody saw me. If anybody saw a girl with black hair, a kerchief on her head, a skinny child. . . . One said, "Check this house. . . . People are dying there on typhus. Maybe she's there."
>
> The house was already on fire. People were on fire. He went behind the barn, he found me there. He grabbed me, and he's carrying me on his back. He was carrying a rifle. . . . He carried whatever food he could . . . some clothing. . . . And they wanted to kill me, the people, the partisans. . . . I heard them say, "Kill her. We're not gonna take her with us. . . . If she's alive, and you gonna leave her, she knows that we are partisans. They're going to look for us."

German soldiers walk through the streets of the Warsaw ghetto in 1944. After the Warsaw Ghetto Uprising, Nazi soldiers razed the area and set fire to the buildings.

> He said, "No. If you want to kill my daughter, the bullet has to go through me."[7]

Of the six hundred who escaped during the uprising, many were hunted down and captured again or killed. Only ninety lived to see the end of the war. Florence was one of the lucky ones.

In the bigger ghettos, revolt was more difficult. The biggest uprising occurred in 1943 in Warsaw, the largest Nazi ghetto. Brave Jews held off the Nazis and their deportation trains for nearly a month, from April 19 until May 16.

In the end, however, the Germans set the ghetto on fire. People died in the flames, were shot, or were captured and sent to the death camps. Zivia Lubetkin, one of the few who escaped during the revolt, described how the children suffered along with their parents:

> The enemy set fire to the ghetto. . . . With their last ounce of strength the Jews ran through the burning rubble in search of shelter. The fire forced them out of their hiding-places and underground bunkers. Many were burnt alive or suffocated from the smoke. Men, women and children sprang from the bowels of the earth clutching their last bits of food, pots and bedding. Babies were held at their mothers' breasts. Older children were dragged behind their parents, with a questioning look of pain and confusion in their eyes as they cried out for help.[8]

For most of the children of Warsaw and the other ghettos, the cries went unanswered. By August 6, 1944, the last ghetto was liquidated. One year later, the war would be over, though that wouldn't matter to the thousands who had died.

Living with the Memories

Hitler did not succeed in murdering all the Jews of Europe. But he did kill two-thirds of them, including 1.5 million children. Those who did survive witnessed unspeakable horrors. The children who lived through the ghettos also

This picture of the child survivors of Auschwitz-Birkenau was taken on the day Soviet soldiers liberated the camp, January 27, 1945. The children here are wearing striped adult uniforms on top of their own clothing.

endured the camps. How did thcy live with the horrible memory of such brutal inhumanity and such great pain?

More than forty years after being liberated, Emanuel Tanay, who became a psychologist, still could not discuss the Holocaust without strong emotion. He explained:

> There is the resistance . . . a lot of ambivalence . . . and fear and difficulty in talking about [the time under Nazi domination]. Survivors are reluctant to talk even to each other about these experiences. Because they are, you know, there are certain experiences if I try to tell you about it, I would break down crying.[9]

Some children who lived through the terrible time felt anger and hate. Ruth Webber, only ten at liberation, had witnessed a lifetime of tragedy:

> I was very bitter after the war, towards everybody. How they allowed me to . . . go through such misery for so long. . . . And I was terribly angry at everything and everybody. Because nobody even cared after I survived, that I survived. . . . So after surviving all this—and, my God, the thoughts, the hate that I had, the things that I was going to do to the Germans for doing these things to us. It's awesome for a child to even think about these—you know, I, I'm even afraid to think about them now myself. I was going to be a butcher. The things that I was going to do to revenge.[10]

Ruth Webber overcame the thirst for revenge by becoming grateful for her survival: "Actually, with the help of mother to try to forget the past, I realized that living a normal life and continue being to be able to, to feel and enjoy, that I was not destroyed."[11]

For a long time, Eve Wagszul Rich felt guilt that she survived and her father did not:

> [The Germans] killed [my father] in front of my eyes. . . . I didn't cry. I didn't scream. I just ran around the kitchen and I got outside. . . . When I think of that moment I can't understand that I didn't take time to make sure that my father is indeed dead. . . . I just cannot explain that and I have a lot of guilt about it and to this day I think about it.[12]

Wagszul overcame the guilt with a reason to continue living:

> The only explanation that I could give you and I have given maybe to myself is that the will of surviving was so strong that I couldn't think of him. I wanted to live for a better world or to tell the story. I was always afraid that all the suffering would be forgotten and there's nobody going to be there to tell the story.[13]

To tell the story was a reason to press through the difficult memories. Emanuel Tanay found the same motivation: "During the war, one of . . . the forces that kept me was the idea that I will tell the world what happened. That, I . . . sort of had a mission. I have to survive because at least somebody has to tell the world what happened."[14]

Tanay, Webber, Wagszul, and the other children who survived the ghettos have told the world what happened. In books, diaries, memoirs, and interviews, they have shared their stories. They have helped others understand the brutality and the kindness of which people are capable. They have shown that it is possible to overcome evil with good. In so doing, they have made certain that no one will ever forget the Holocaust.

Timeline

1939

September 1—German invasion of Poland begins World War II.

October 8—First ghetto is established in Piotrkow Trybunalski, Poland, sixteen miles south of Lodz.

October 28—Piotrkow ghetto is sealed.

November 23—Jews in German-occupied Poland are required to wear the Star of David.

December 20—Radomsko, Poland, ghetto is established.

1940

February 8—Jews of Lodz, Poland, are ordered into a ghetto, the second-largest ghetto.

April 30—Lodz ghetto is sealed.

May 10—Germany invades France, Belgium, Holland, and Luxembourg.

October 12—Warsaw, Poland, ghetto is established, the largest ghetto.

October 14—Mass deportations of Jews from the Reich to ghettos in Kovno, Lodz, Minsk, and Riga begin.

November 15—Warsaw ghetto is sealed.

1941

March 3—Krakow, Poland, ghetto is established.

March 20—Krakow ghetto is sealed.

March 31—Kielce, Poland, ghetto is established.

June 22—Germany invades Soviet Union.

July 10—Kovno, Poland, ghetto is established.

August—Ghettos of Lvov and Bialystok are established in Belorussia.

September 6—Vilna ghetto is established in Lithuania.

November—Grodno ghetto is established in Belorussia.

November 24—Theresienstadt ghetto is established in Czechoslovakia.

1942

January 16—Jews from Lodz are sent to Chelmno death camp.

January 20—Wannsee Conference coordinates the "final solution."

February—Evacuation of ghettos in Poland begins.

March–October—Residents of ghettos are sent to death camps.

April 4—Lachwa ghetto is established in Belorussia.

May—Systematic gassing begins at Auschwitz.

June 23—Systematic gassing begins at Treblinka.

July—Mass deportations of Warsaw Jews to Treblinka death camp begin.

August 22–24—Kielce ghetto is liquidated and Jews are deported to Treblinka.

October 14–21—Liquidation of Piotrkow ghetto begins.

September 2—First ghetto uprising occurs in Lachwa.

1943

January 18—First armed resistance occurs in Warsaw ghetto.

March 13—Grodno is declared *Judenrein*—cleansed of Jews.

March 14—Krakow ghetto is liquidated.

April 19–May 16—Warsaw ghetto revolts.

June 11—Heinrich Himmler orders liquidation of all Polish ghettos.

June 21—Himmler orders liquidation of all remaining Soviet ghettos.

Summer—Armed resistance takes place in Bedzin, Bialystok, Czestochowa, Lvov, and Tarnów ghettos.

August 16–23—Jews are deported from Bialystok ghetto.

September 1—Armed revolt occurs in Vilna ghetto; a few escape.

Fall—Ghettos of Minsk, Vilna, and Riga are liquidated.

1944

April–July—Jews in Hungary are placed in ghettos and then deported to Auschwitz.

August 1—Soviet army liberates Kovno.

August 6—Lodz is last ghetto liquidated.

November 24—Last Jews in Piotrkow are evacuated to camps.

1945

January 16—Piotrkow is liberated by Soviet army.

May 8—German army surrenders unconditionally, ending World War II.

Chapter Notes

Chapter 1

Creating the Ghettos

1. Harold Zissman, *The Warriors: My Life as a Jewish Soviet Partisan* (Syracuse, NY: Syracuse University Press, 2005), p. 17.
2. Harold Zissman, *Oral History Interview*, United States Holocaust Memorial Museum (USHMM) Archives RG-50.030*0318.
3. Edward Lessing, *Oral History Interview,* USHMM Archives RG-50.030* 0127.
4. Helene Baraf, *Oral History Interview*, USHMM Archives RG-50.030* 0015.
5. Emanuel Tanay, *Oral History Interview*, USHMM Archives RG-50.042* 0027, Acc. 1994, A.447.
6. Madeline Deutsch, *Oral History Interview*, USHMMArchives RG-50.549.01* 0027.
7. Ibid.
8. Regina Hamburger Bomba, *Oral History Interview*, USHMM Archives RG-50.030*0034.
9. Nesse Galperin Godin, *Oral History Interview*, USHMM Archives RG-50.106*0105, Acc. 1998, A.0143.
10. Rochelle Blackman Slivka, *Oral History Interview*, USHMM Archives RG-50.549.02*0026, Acc. 1998, A.0229.

Chapter 2

Relocation, Isolation, and Imprisonment

1. Amalie Petranker Salsitz, *Oral History Interview*, USHMM Archives RG-50.030*0198.
2. Ibid.
3. Nina Kaleska, *Oral History Interview*, USHMM Archives RG-50.030* 0101.
4. Michael Etkind, from a manuscript sent to Martin Gilbert and cited in Martin Gilbert, *The Boys: The Story of 732 Young Concentration Camp Survivors* (New York, NY: Macmillan, 1998), p. 76.
5. Irena Aronowicz, "Children During the Holocaust," Holocaust Encyclopedia, n.d., http://www.ushmm.org/wlc/article.php?lang=en&ModuleId=10007285 (accessed November 30, 2017).

6. Lily Margules, *Oral History Interview*, USHMM Archives RG-50.030* 0150.
7. Petranker Salsitz.
8. Ben Helfgott, cited in "Piotrkow Trybunalski Ghetto," Aktion Reinhard Camps, 2006, http://www.deathcamps.org/occupation/piotrkow%20ghetto.html (accessed November 30, 2017).
9. Sonia Heidocovsky Zissman, *Oral History Interview*, USHMM Archives RG-50.030*0332.
10. Helfgott.
11. Emanuel Tanay, "Experience as a Survivor," University of Michigan-Dearborn Voice/Vision Holocaust Survivor Oral History Archive, March 16, 1987, http://holocaust.umd.umich.edu/interview.php?D=tanay&section=20 (accessed November 30, 2017).
12. Abraham Malnik, *Oral History Interview*, USHMM Archives RG-50.030* 0145.
13. Tanay.
14. Emanuel Tanay, *Oral History Interview*, USHMM Archives RG-50.042*0027, Acc. 1994, A.447.
15. Tosha Bialer, in Nora Levin, *The Holocaust: The Destruction of European Jewry, 1933–1945* (New York, NY: Thomas Y. Crowell, 1968), p. 208; From Tosha Bialer's article "Beyond the Wall (Life—and Death—in Warsaw's Ghetto)," originally published in *Collier's*, February 20 and 27, 1943.
16. David Lieberman, *Oral History Interview*, USHMM Archives RG-50.030*0198.
17. Yitskhok Rudashevski, diary entry for September 6, 1941, in Alexandra Zapruder, ed., *Salvaged Pages: Young Writers' Diaries of the Holocaust* (New Haven, CT: Yale University Press, 2002), pp. 199–200.

Chapter 3

"Life Goes On"

1. Emanuel Tanay, "Experience as a Survivor," University of Michigan-Dearborn Voice/Vision Holocaust Survivor Oral History Archive, March 16, 1987, http://holocaust.umd.umich.edu/interview.php?D=tanay&section=20 (accessed November 30, 2017).
2. Justice Thomas Buergenthal, *Oral History Interview*, USHMM Archives RG-50.030*0198.

3. Eva Rozencwajig, *Oral History Interview*, USHMM Archives RG-50.030*0225.
4. Hanka Ziegler, cited in "Piotrkow Trybunalski Ghetto," Aktion Reinhard Camps, 2006, http://www.deathcamps.org/occupation/piotrkow%20ghetto.html (accessed November 30, 2017).
5. Stefan Ernest, from his memoirs cited in Barbara Engelking, *Holocaust and Memory: The Experience of the Holocaust and Its Consequences: An Investigation Based on Personal Narratives*, trans. Emma Harris (London, UK: Leicester University Press, 2001), p. 116.
6. Claudia Royter Liberchuk, *Oral History Interview*, USHMM Archives RG-50.030*0484.
7. Florence Gittelman Eisen, *Oral History Interview*, USHMM Archives RG-50.030*0260.
8. Tanay.
9. Nelly Zygler Cesana, "Warsaw Ghetto Survivor Recalls Hunger, Fear and Grief," *Jewish News Weekly of Northern California*, May 2, 2003, https://www.jweekly.com/2003/05/02/warsaw-ghetto-survivor-recalls-hunger-fear-and-grief (accessed November 30, 2017).
10. Chaim Benzion Cale, "Children During the Holocaust," Holocaust Encyclopedia, n.d., http://www.ushmm.org/wlc/article.php?lang=en& ModuleId=10007287 (accessed November 30, 2017).
11. Dawid Sierakowiak, "Children During the Holocaust," Holocaust Encyclopedia, n.d., http://www.ushmm.org/wlc/article.php?lang=en&ModuleId=10007294 (accessed November 30, 2017).
12. Sara Rachela Plagier, "Children During the Holocaust," Holocaust Encyclopedia, http://www.ushmm.org/wlc/article.php?lang=en&ModuleId=10007293 (accessed November 30, 2017).
13. Anonymous girl diarist from the Lodz ghetto, "Diary Excerpts," Holocaust Encyclopedia, https://www.ushmm.org/wlc/en/article.php?ModuleId=10007284 (accessed November 30, 2017).
14. Sonia Heidocovsky Zissman, *Oral History Interview*, USHMM Archives RG-50.030*0332.
15. Buergenthal.
16. Israel Unikowski, "Children During the Holocaust," Holocaust Encyclopedia, http://www.ushmm.org/wlc/article.php?lang=en&ModuleId=10007296 (accessed November 30, 2017).
17. Tanay.
18. Ibid.
19. Cale.

Chapter 4
Finding a Way to Survive

1. Dawid Sierakowiak, "Children During the Holocaust," Holocaust Encyclopedia, http://www.ushmm.org/wlc/article.php?lang=en&ModuleId=10007294 (accessed November 30, 2017).
2. Eve Wagszul Rich, *Oral History Interview*, USHMM Archives RG-50.030*0188.
3. Abraham Malnik, *Oral History Interview*, USHMM Archives RG-50.030* 0145.
4. Blanka Rothschild, *Oral History Interview*, USHMM Archives RG-50.030* 0281.
5. Lily Margoles, *Oral History Interview*, USHMM Archives RG-50.030* 0150.
6. Sierakowiak.
7. Karolina Dresler, "Children During the Holocaust," Holocaust Encyclopedia, http://www.ushmm.org/wlc/article.php?lang=en&ModuleId=10007288 (accessed November 30, 2017).
8. Rut Berlinska, "Children During the Holocaust," Holocaust Encyclopedia, http://www.ushmm.org/wlc/article.php?lang=en&ModuleId= 10007286 (accessed November 30, 2017).
9. Yitskhok Rudashevski, diary entry, cited in Deborah Dwork, *The Holocaust: A History* (New York, NY: W. W. Norton, 2002), p. 191.
10. Beno Helmer, *Oral History Interview*, USHMM Archives RG-50.030* 0093.
11. David Lieberman, *Oral History Interview*, USHMM Archives RG-50.030* 0198.
12. David J. Selznick, *Oral History Interview*, USHMM Archives RG-50.030* 0211.
13. Ibid.
14. Helmer.
15. Rothschild.
16. Ibid.
17. Thomas Toivi Blatt, *Oral History Interview*, USHMM Archives RG-50.030*0028.
18. Sonia Heidocovsky Zissman, *Oral History Interview*, USHMM Archives RG-50.030*332.
19. Ibid.
20. Rothschild.
21. Sara Rachela Plagier, "Children During the Holocaust," Holocaust Encyclopedia, http://www.ushmm.org/wlc/article.php?lang=en&ModuleId=10007293 (accessed November 30, 2017).

22. Hanka Ziegler, cited in "Piotrkow Trybunalski Ghetto," Aktion Reinhard Camps, 2006, http://www.deathcamps.org/occupation/piotrkow%20ghetto.html (accessed November 30, 2017).
23. Judith Meisel, "Personal Histories," United States Holocaust Memorial Museum Online Exhibit, https://www.ushmm.org/wlc/en/media_oi.php?ModuleId=0&MediaId=1155 (accessed November 30, 2017).
24. Charlene Perlmutter Schiff, *Oral History Interview*, USHMM Archives RG-50.030*0203.

Chapter 5

Clinging to Hope

1. William J. Lowenberg, *Oral History Interview*, USHMM Archives RG-50.030*0139.
2. Inge Auerbacher,"Children During the Holocaust," Holocaust Encyclopedia, https://www.ushmm.org/wlc/en/idcard.php?ModuleId=10006364 (accessed November 30, 2017).
3. Ibid.
4. Oskar Rosenfeld, Lodz Chronicle entry, cited in Deborah Dwork, *The Holocaust: A History* (New York, NY: W. W. Norton, 2002), pp. 190–191.
5. Emanuel Tanay, "Experience as a Survivor," University of Michigan-Dearborn Voice/Vision Holocaust Survivor Oral History Archive, March 16, 1987, hhttp://holocaust.umd.umich.edu/interview.php?D=tanay&section=20 (accessed November 30, 2017).
6. Ephraim Dekel, *Between Our Yesterdays and Our Tomorrows*, p. 121, cited in "Schools in the Ghetto," *Children in the Ghetto*, http://ghetto.galim.org.il/eng/school/writing.html (accessed May 28, 2008).
7. Yitskhok Rudashevski, *Diary of the Vilna Ghetto, June 1941–April 1943* (Tel Aviv, Israel: Kibbutz Lohamei Haghetaot, 1973), cited in United States Holocaust Memorial Museum, *Fifty Years Ago: Revolt Amid the Darkness* (Washington, DC: USHMM, 1993), p. 61.
8. Avraham Golub, diary entry, cited in Deborah Dwork, *The Holocaust: A History* (New York, NY: W. W. Norton, 2002), p. 223.
9. Hana Fuchs Krasa, *Oral History Interview*, USHMM Archives RG-50.030* 0479.
10. Edgar Krasa, *Oral History Interview*, USHMM Archives RG-50.030* 0478.
11. Ibid.
12. Ibid.

13. Ibid.
14. Ibid.
15. Ibid.
16. Hana Fuchs Krasa.
17. Miriam Goldberg, "Children During the Holocaust," Holocaust Encyclopedia, http://www.ushmm.org/wlc/article.php?lang=en&ModuleId=10007289 (November 30, 2017).

Chapter 6

From Ghettos to Death Camps

1. Thomas Toivi Blatt, *Oral History Interview*, USHMM Archives RG-50.030*0028.
2. Abraham Malnik, *Oral History Interview*, USHMM Archives RG-50.030* 0145.
3. Anonymous, *Oral History Interview*, USHMM Archives RG-50.030* XXX.
4. Ibid.
5. Yitskhok Rudashevski, *Diary of the Vilna Ghetto, June 1941–April 1943* (Tel Aviv, Israel: Kibbutz Lohamei Haghetaot, 1973), cited in United States Holocaust Memorial Museum, *Fifty Years Ago: Revolt Amid the Darkness* (Washington, DC: USHMM, 1993), p. 64.
6. Emanuel Tanay, "Experience as a Survivor," University of Michigan-Dearborn Voice/Vision Holocaust Survivor Oral History Archive, March 16, 1987, http://holocaust.umd.umich.edu/interview.php?D=tanay&section=20 (accessed November 30, 2017).
7. Rudashevski.
8. Ibid.
9. Malnik.
10. Tanay.
11. Amalie Petranker Salsitz, *Oral History Interview*, USHMM Archives RG-50.030*0198.
12. Ibid.
13. Sara Rachela Plagier, "Children During the Holocaust," Holocaust Encyclopedia, http://www.ushmm.org/wlc/article.php?lang=en&ModuleId=10007293 (accessed November 30, 2017).
14. Brigitte Friedmann Altman, "Personal Stories," Holocaust Encyclopedia, https://www.ushmm.org/wlc/en/media_oi.php?ModuleId=0&MediaId=2969 (accessed November 30, 2017).
15. Thomas Buergenthal, *Oral History Interview*, USHMM Archives RG-50.030*0046.

16. Petranker Salsitz.
17. Eve Wagszul Rich, *Oral History Interview*, USHMM Archives RG-50.030* 0188.
18. Henny Fletcher Aronson, *Oral History Interview*, USHMM Archives RG- 50.030*0290.
19. Malnik.
20. David Lieberman, *Oral History Interview*, USHMM Archives RG-50.030* 0198.
21. Cecilie Klein-Pollack, *Oral History Interview*, USHMM Archives RG-50.042*0018.
22. Abraham Lewent, *Oral History Interview*, USHMM Archives RG-50.030* 0130, Acc. 1989, H, 0344.
23. Sol Lurie, *Oral History Interview*, USHMM Archives RG-50.030*0141.
24. Ibid.
25. Jakub Lapides, "Children During the Holocaust," Holocaust Encyclopedia, http://www.ushmm.org/wlc/article.php?lang=en&ModuleId= 10007291 (accessed November 30, 2017).
26. Chaim Kozienicki, "Children During the Holocaust," Holocaust Encyclopedia, http://www.ushmm.org/wlc/article.php?lang=en&ModuleId=10007290 (accessed November 30, 2017).

Chapter 7

Liquidation in Full

1. Abraham Malnik, *Oral History Interview*, USHMM Archives RG-50.030*0145.
2. Aaron Elster, *Oral History Interview*, USHMM Archives Acc. 1998. A. 0017.
3. Emanuel Tanay, "Experience as a Survivor," University of Michigan-Dearborn Voice/Vision Holocaust Survivor Oral History Archive, March 16, 1987, http://holocaust.umd.umich.edu/interview.php?D=tanay&section=20 (accessed November 30, 2017).
4. Irena Sendlerowa, Association of Children of the Holocaust in Poland, http://www.dzieciholocaustu.org.pl/szab58.php?s=en_sendlerowa.php (accessed November 30, 2017).
5. Ibid.
6. Lily Margules, *Oral History Interview*, USHMM Archives RG-50.030*0150.
7. Florence Gittelman Eisen, *Oral History Interview*, USHMM Archives RG-50.030*0260.

8. Zivia Lubetkin, *In the Days of Destruction and Revolt*, trans. Ishai Tubbin (Tel Aviv, Israel: Ghetto Fighters' House, 1981), cited in United States Holocaust Memorial Museum, *Fifty Years Ago: Revolt Amid the Darkness* (Washington, DC: USHMM, 1993), p. 203.
9. Emanuel Tanay, "Experience as a Survivor," University of Michigan-Dearborn Voice/Vision Holocaust Survivor Oral History Archive, March 16, 1987,http://holocaust.umd.umich.edu/interview.php?D=tanay&section=20 (accessed November 30, 2017).
10. Ruth Webber, "Personal Histories," United States Holocaust Memorial Museum Online Exhibit, https://www.ushmm.org/wlc/en/media_oi.php?ModuleId=0&MediaId=5722 (November 30, 2017).
11. Ibid.
12. Eve Wagszul Rich, *Oral History Interview*, United States Holocaust Memorial Museum (USHMM) Archives RG-50.030*0188.
13. Ibid.
14. Tanay.

Glossary

Aktion The operation in which Jews were harassed or rounded up and sent to work camps or death camps.

barricade A barrier thrown together out of whatever is on hand.

brigade A group of people organized for a specific work assignment.

gendarmes Armed policemen.

Gestapo Geheime Staatspolizei, literally "secret state police," or the Nazi police.

Judenrat The council of Jewish elders in Nazi-occupied cities that was responsible for order in the ghettos and for communicating and carrying out German orders.

liquidation Term Nazis used to mean "complete destruction." Sometimes the term was used to describe an action in which only some residents were either killed outright or transported to a death camp. In this case, the action was usually a step toward total destruction of the ghetto.

partisan Person belonging to a group of people, often Soviet soldiers and ghetto escapees, who hid from the Nazis and fought them in the forests of the Soviet Union and Poland.

ration The amount of an item that was allowed. In the ghettos, food was rationed; each person was allowed only a certain, very small amount.

Schutzstaffel (SS) Military-like organization. Members of the SS served as camp guards and police.

selection Term used by Nazis for the process of identifying and gathering Jews for a specific purpose: for a work crew, for deportation, or for death.

sledge A vehicle mounted on runners instead of wheels, often used to pull people or objects over ice and snow.

truncheon A rubber club or short stick used as a weapon by police.

Further Reading

Books

Bornstein, Michael, and Debbie Bornstein Holinstat. *Survivors Club: The True Story of a Very Young Prisoner of Auschwitz*. New York, NY: Farrar, Straus & Giroux, 2017.

Deem, James M. *The Prisoners of Breendonk: Personal Histories from a World War II Concentration Camp*. New York, NY: HMH Books for Young Readers, 2015.

Gruenbaum, Michael. *Somewhere There Is Still a Star.* New York, NY: Aladdin, 2015.

Iturbe, Antonio, and Lilit Thwaites (trans.). *The Librarian of Auschwitz.* New York, NY: Henry Holt & Co., 2017.

Mazzeo, Tilar J. *Irena's Children: The Extraordinary Story of the Woman Who Saved 2,500 Children from the Warsaw Ghetto*. New York, NY: Gallery Books, 2016.

Shackleton, Kath. *Survivors of the Holocaust*. London, UK: Hachette, 2016.

Yolen, Jane. *Mapping the Bones*. New York, NY: Philomel Books, 2018.

Websites

BBC—The Holocaust Year by Year

http://www.bbc.co.uk/timelines/z86nfg8

An interactive timeline displaying the events of each year of the Holocaust.

History Channel Online

http://www.history.com/topics/world-war-ii/the-holocaust

The online branch of the History Channel offers videos and articles about the Holocaust more generally.

How Stuff Works: Stuff You Missed in History Class

https://www.missedinhistory.com/tags/world-war-ii.htm

A plethora of podcasts on all aspects of World War II.

The United States Holocaust Memorial Museum
www.ushmm.org/learn/students/the-holocaust-a-learning-site-for-students
The museum, located in Washington, DC, has a vast online archive of survivor interviews, informational articles, videos, and images.

Films

Defiance, dir. Edward Zwick, 2008.

"Escape from Auschwitz," April 29, 2008, *Secrets of the Dead: Unearthing History*, PBS, television program.

Index